Entertaining
with
Michael Barry

Oven temp/ p. 6

Entertaining with Michael Barry

EBURY PRESS
London

Published by Ebury Press
National Magazine House
72 Broadwick Street
London W1V 2BP

First impression 1979

ISBN 0 85223 152 0

Designer Derek Morrison
Line drawings by Elaine Handley
Cover photograph by Roger Tuff

Cover photograph shows
Guacamole (page 49), Paella (page 32),
Orange fool (page 63), Pavlova (page 70)

The author and publisher would like to thank the following for
their help in providing props for the cover photograph:

Dickins & Jones Ltd (china, glassware and cruet)
Denby Tableware Ltd (white cutlery)
The Inside Out Shops Ltd (table)

Filmset and printed in Great Britain by
BAS Printers Limited, Over Wallop, Hampshire
and bound by
William Brendon and Son Limited, Tiptree, Essex

Contents

Handy Cookery Charts

CONVERSION TO METRIC MEASUREMENTS

The metric measures in this book are based on a 25 g unit instead of the ounce (28.35 g). Slight adjustments to this basic conversion standard were necessary in some recipes to achieve satisfactory cooking results.

If you want to convert your own recipes from imperial to metric, we suggest you use the same 25 g unit, and use 600 ml in place of 1 pint, with the British Standard 5-ml and 15-ml spoons replacing the old variable teaspoons and table-spoons. These adaptations will sometimes give a slightly smaller recipe quantity and may require a shorter cooking time.

Note Sets of British Standard metric measuring spoons are available in the following sizes — 2.5 ml, 5 ml, 10 ml and 15 ml.

When measuring milk it is more convenient to use the exact conversion of 568 ml (1 pint).

For more general reference, the following tables will be helpful.

METRIC CONVERSION SCALE

Imperial	LIQUID Exact conversion	Recommended ml	Imperial	SOLID Exact conversion	Recommended g
$\frac{1}{4}$ pint	142 ml	150 ml	1 oz	28.35 g	25 g
$\frac{1}{2}$ pint	284 ml	300 ml	2 oz	56.7 g	50 g
1 pint	568 ml	600 ml	4 oz	113.4 g	100 g
$1\frac{1}{2}$ pints	851 ml	900 ml	8 oz	226.8 g	225 g
$1\frac{3}{4}$ pints	992 ml	1 litre	12 oz	340.2 g	350 g
			14 oz	397.0 g	400 g
			16 oz (1 lb)	453.6 g	450 g

For quantities of $1\frac{3}{4}$ pints and over, litres and fractions of a litre have been used.

1 kilogram (kg) equals 2.2 lb.

Note Follow either the metric or the imperial measures in the recipes as they are not interchangeable.

OVEN TEMPERATURE CHART

°C	°F	Gas mark
110	225	$\frac{1}{4}$
130	250	$\frac{1}{2}$
140	275	1
150	300	2
170	325	3
180	350	4
190	375	5
200	400	6
220	425	7
230	450	8
240	475	9

RECIPE FOR RELAXED ENTERTAINING

30 ml (2 tbsp) bath oil
45 litres (10 gallons) hot water
1 hostess
1 large towel, heated

Add the bath oil to the water and test that the temperature is not so hot as to damage the skin. Carefully peel the body and ensure that the hair is piled up safely on top of the head. Immerse gently in the water, stretch out fully and leave to marinate for 20 minutes. Wash carefully, using fine soap, rinse, remove from the water, and wrap in a hot towel. Garnish attractively and serve cool, with a dash of sauce.

Timing: 60 minutes beforehand.

Introduction

The recipe on the previous page is probably the most important one in the book. Like all my recipes, it does not have to be followed to the absolute letter – you can experiment a little if you like, but it is vital to start roughly an hour beforehand.

Treating yourself to a leisurely bath before the guests arrive is sound advice because the secret of crafty, confident entertaining is to relax and have a good time *yourself* – even though you are the one that's giving the party. A calm beginning is pretty important for that (even if it only gives you time to remember the three things you have forgotten to do). Make sure you get your share of attention so you don't look flustered and anxious, or your guests, no matter how good the actual cooking is, just aren't going to enjoy the evening that much. A happy, confident hostess is the secret of success, both socially and gastronomically. Balancing the 'texture' and 'flavour' of the occasion – achieving a happy harmonious atmosphere – is quite as important as balancing the texture and flavour of the meal.

The other golden rule of entertaining is to do whatever you do, and serve whatever you serve, with *style*. Fish fingers with flair are far better than Apple strudel with apologies. In the last resort, however good the cooking, people come to see, meet and be with *you* – remember that! The purpose of this book is to make sure they get a chance to enjoy as much of that company as they can and still think they are eating in the home of one of the greatest cooks of the western world!

All my recipes are designed to take the least amount of effort for the maximum taste result. Some of them cut a few corners that are unusual; all of them, I hope, do not show it in the result when you and your family and friends come to eat it. The crafty part is not what you do – or rather don't have to do – when you are preparing the meal, but what they don't know and certainly don't have to find out about in the dining room.

In the recipe file that starts on page 21, you will find main courses given first. This is because you'll probably find it easier to build your meal round the chief course. To help you plan your menu, alternative suggestions are given at the foot of each main course for suitable starters and puddings to go with it, depending on the degree of formality or casualness you are aiming at. Recipes for these starters and desserts follow the main course section. Do remember that these suggestions are only suggestions, and as with all things, what feels right for you and your guests is the right menu to serve. But I have chosen the meals to involve a minimum of last-minute work and a maximum of interest and flavour, texture and contrast in the meal itself.

Later on comes a section on special types of parties, ranging from a posh buffet for forty people to an Indian meal for six that you can prepare without going near a take-away. I've also included that great ice-breaker, golden bubbling Swiss cheese fondue as the basis for a 'getting to know you' party and some ideas for a barbecue on a summer evening as the last of the light fades from a clear blue sky.

A note on equipment

Your ordinary pots, pans and casseroles, dishes and bowls will be fine for easy entertaining in every way, but there is one piece of equipment that I think is pretty essential and that is some kind of blender. One of the super new food processors is best if you are lucky or rich enough to have one. The Magimix is probably and rightly the best known. It'll do anything from making pastry or chips for you to liquidizing a soup. But ordinary blenders with a litre-sized plastic goblet are invaluable in many ways. Moulinex do one with a coffee grinder attachment that will make breadcrumbs or chopped nuts as well.

The only other essential tools are two *sharp* knives, one big one, one small one. You only cut the food, not yourself, with a good sharp blade, so make sure they stay sharp as you use them. Stainless steel is best; not only does it stay sharp longer but it doesn't stain and look grotty either if you happen to put the knife down without washing it immediately.

The last important and perhaps the craftiest tool of all is a whisk. Look at the drawing and go and find one that looks like it. No other shape does the job half as well. This particular whisk seems to have the ability to blend any sauce smoothly, beat perfect meringues, whip cream like snow, and save your reputation countless times. Keep looking until you find one – *really.*

Dinner Parties

To start with, setting the scene. The physical bits, the surroundings and so on, are quite important and it doesn't matter whether you are having an intimate dinner for two with candlelight and roses on the table, or putting on a fairly grand dinner for eight. Nor does it matter whether your crockery is finest porcelain or supermarket stoneware – the effect you achieve can still be successful if you bear in mind the following points.

Unless you have got a pretty spacious kitchen, or have no choice at all as to where you entertain, it is better to eat somewhere where you are not actually cooking. It avoids the necessity of trying to cook a meal at the same time as keeping the kitchen like a colour supplement ad. And it gives you a private moment to make sure that everything is looking and tasting quite the way it ought to before it actually arrives on the table. It stops even the most convivial of guests from wandering over – picking up saucepan lids – poking about – and generally upsetting your air of calm confidence. So, eat somewhere other than the kitchen, and ideally – somewhere where you can lay the table well in advance. Not too far from the kitchen though; it's not a lot of fun if you have a five-minute walk between courses in order to get something from the stove or the oven, or if you have forgotten the salt!

Tables and seating plans

As to the table itself, an oval or oblong or square one is ideal. Unless you have got a lot of space and are a real expert at seating people, round ones always seem to me to be more trouble than they are worth. The seating plan, so often a cause of worry, is very simple if you remember these rules: the host and hostess should, if possible, sit opposite each other with the most important female guest on the host's right and the most important male guest on the hostess's right. The second most important female guest should be on the host's left and the second most important male guest on the hostess's left.

This placing goes on right the way down the table on each side, over-lapping men and women

as you go if you have more than six people sitting down to dinner. You will find it keeps husbands and wives within speaking distance, but not next to each other or directly opposite (except for the host and hostess of course). It mixes the sexes without aggravation and means you can work out in advance who is going to be where. As to who *are* the most important guests – you will have to decide that for yourself of course, but if you are sticking to any kind of old-fashioned etiquette, older people, guests in the house for the first time and people with a special status, normally take precedence. You probably won't want to bother with name cards for any but the most formal party, but think out a seating plan beforehand.

Covering up!

I know it's not everybody's taste, but I think nothing looks quite so nice on a table as a tablecloth and matching table napkins. Mats, runners or bamboo sections can be pretty and if you have got them and like them, please use them. But for me nothing looks quite so good as the basis for an appetising meal as a fine tablecloth with a small centrepiece of flowers or candles. *Not* a large centrepiece please – firstly you won't have anywhere to put the dishes down, and secondly, your guests will have to peer round or through it in order to speak to each other. A couple of small candelabra a third of the way down from each end of the table is a good alternative. I have a soft spot for flowers; I think they add a touch of naturalness to even the most formal and grand of dinner parties. A couple of garden flowers often do much better in this respect than a formal arrangement, however lovely or expensive.

Don't take too long dressing up the table at this stage; the important thing is not how it looks in its pristine condition, but how well it is going to serve the purpose of being the basis for a lively and delicious dinner party. In the centre, make sure you have got enough heatproof mats for any hot dishes you are bringing in and that the salt, pepper, butter dish and any other accompaniments you are likely to be using are ready to

Top Formal place setting. *Bottom* Informal place setting.

hand. Unless this is going to be an entirely cold meal, it is usually wise to lay a place mat in front of each place with the cutlery arranged on either side of it.

Place settings

The rules for laying out cutlery are very simple. Start on the outside with the equipment you are going to use first; soup spoon if you are going to serve soup, fish knife and fork if it is going to be fish, for example, and work inwards until you get to the end of the savoury courses. Sweet courses have their cutlery laid above the place mat; left hand tools, *ie* forks, nearer the mat than right hand tools. On the far left of the cutlery, put a

bread plate with a bread knife on it or across it, and on the right hand side of the place mat goes the glass.

If you are going to serve more than one kind of wine, you need a glass for each kind – tall and thin for white, shorter and fatter for red (see pages 89–90 for shapes of glasses). I usually include a water glass as some people may not want wine and many people enjoy a glass of water to clear the palate and refresh themselves. If you haven't got special knives and forks for special courses do not worry, a small knife and fork will do just as well for a fish course as a specially shaped piece of equipment.

Try to make sure that all the cutlery 'goes'

together, although it does not have to be from perfectly matching sets; the same applies to the crockery. In many continental countries, it is quite the thing for each guest to have forks, knives and plates that are entirely different from his neighbours', as a matter of interest and for variation in design. I am not suggesting we go as far as that, but if you have to use more than one set of plates, try and do it as though you meant to do it – alternating the sets – rather than giving everyone the same and keeping the odd one for yourself in the hope that no one will notice.

While all this may sound terribly formal, it is really just the basic set of rules. If you want to go to the other extreme and serve one course and hand round a basket of fruit to follow, one knife and fork is going to be fine. You have to suit the setting to the style and the mood you are trying to create. You don't *have* to have Georgian silver for a grand dinner party – people respond very well to simplicity.

The groaning (side)board

Sideboards – although we now tend to use them for other reasons – were originally intended to make life easier at the dinner table. It is a device I am all in favour of bringing back, even if it is in its modified form of the heated food trolley. If you can manage it, get as much of the meal as won't spoil from being set out, into the dining room early, together with the plates and equipment you will need to serve it. Put them on a side table, or trolley, or sideboard – whichever suits you better. Make sure you leave a little space for the clearing off job at the same time, if you are planning to stay in the dining room or area after the meal. It is often easier to carve, for example, on a side table, where the occasional and almost inevitable unexpected movements of the joint are more likely to escape your guests' notice.

Don't be afraid, especially on less formal occasions, to serve food from the dish it was cooked in. Nothing brings home the true, authentic scent and savour of Provence more than to see in front of you a rich stew in a French earthenware casserole still crusty and dark from the oven. I am all for real things appearing in real dishes, but do make sure that they look attractive; that the casserole has a sprinkling of fresh green parsley on it, that the dish that has been in the refrigerator has been wiped so that any splashes or smears are taken off. Take advantage wherever you can of the new 'cook-and-serve'

casseroles and saucepans being brought on to the market. Not only do they look good on the table, they save extra washing-up!

Cue lights and music?

There is no doubt that candlelight is the most flattering light there is, both for your guests – especially the female ones – and your food, but unless you have lots of candles, it is unlikely that they will give enough light of their own, so a little background light, preferably indirect, is a good idea. Or have one of those adjustable height overhead lights that you can set at a low level to throw a flattering glow on the face, and put the candles elsewhere, say on the sideboard. Failing this, take advantage of one of the new dimmer switches you can buy, otherwise the effect of the candles will be totally wiped out. If you are eating in daylight, of course, there is no problem, but if it is evening – unless there happens to be a spectacular view – I am a great believer in artificial light. Natural light tends to fade as the evening draws on and the fuss of having to start lighting candles or turning on bright electric lights destroys the atmosphere of the evening. But once again, you must suit your own taste and your own circumstances and home in making these sorts of decisions. There are exceptions to every rule, and an open window on a summer evening with the scent of honeysuckle floating in and a glorious sunset behind, can turn even the most simple of suppers into a stupendous occasion.

One thing I am sure about is music; the sound that ought to be heard at the table is people, talking not playing! There is a place for music when you are entertaining – both before and after the meal – but while you are eating, unless you are the sort of person who has a minstrels' gallery and players to fill it (like in mediaeval banquets), it is better to stick to talk rather than tape! Make sure, in order to achieve this wonderful buzz of conversation, that your guests are close enough together, by the way. I always think people can take over-crowding better than separation. You don't actually mind someone's elbow in your steak and kidney if they are fascinating you with stories about their trip up the Yangtse. Elbow room's not a lot of use if it means you are just slightly out of ear-shot of the most interesting person in the room.

Play it by ear

Before dinner, a little fairly light popular-style music always seems to me to help get a party going, especially with guests who may not know each other too well, or who may be a little uncertain. After dinner though – with the lights down low and the proverbial bottomless coffee pot passing round – you can afford something more mellow and thoughtful. Some not too arduous classical music – Bach or Vivaldi – never seems to offend anybody; or one of the modern classics such as Sinatra, Streisand or Liza Minnelli are my style. If your guests are into 'The Boomtown Rats' then you are going to have to adjust your 'play list' accordingly, but just be sure they really are before you commit yourself.

Stage managing the evening

'The best laid tables gang oft agley . . .' to misquote Robbie Burns – a well known trencherman in his own right. The key to the matter is choosing guests. How many, how to mix them, what to do if *they* start to mix their drinks! As to how many, that is up to you and your capacity both to cook for and look after them. Six or eight is my favourite number, but there are rumours that dinner for two is quite popular and I have got nothing against four. For your convenience, the recipes for dinner parties include two columns of ingredients, the left hand one for four people (you can double it for eight) and the right hand for six people. Remember though that more than eight really does require pretty careful strategic planning and a lot of room – not to mention a very large dining table. Dinner for upwards of twelve *I* think needs a special ingredient called servants, and I really do not recommend undertaking it except buffet style, preferably with someone to help you.

Having decided on the numbers, the key question is how to pick them so that they get on well together. I have only one secret which is always to make sure that amongst the guests is a 'performer' – somebody who enjoys telling stories, being the centre of attention – and who is good at it! Be careful not to invite two 'performers' to the same dinner party unless they happen to be very good friends and used to doing a double act. Also make sure that he or she knows when 'enough is enough' without having to have too sharp a kick on the ankle!

I don't believe in mixing up ages, attitudes or interests too much, unless the people concerned have got a strong common denominator. A young newly married couple may be over-awed by a local celebrity while he or she may in turn be put off by people who do not know anything about them. This does not mean always avoiding any form of potential argument or disagreement amongst your guests, but making sure that all the people you invite together have enough common ground in order to be able to stand up to each other.

Drinks – before and after

Try and make sure that everything's going to be ready about half an hour after your guests are due to arrive. Many of them won't arrive on the dot out of politeness, or because of unforeseen circumstances and it is just frustrating to have everything beginning to spoil as soon as anybody is five minutes late. Half an hour is about right for pre-dinner drinks too and I always think it is important to go quite easy on these.

Make sure you have one or two soft alternatives to alcohol for anybody who doesn't want the hard stuff because they are driving, or for whatever reason; fruit juices and Perrier water are good standbys. For the drinkers, sherry is a pretty universal and acceptable favourite, medium dry usually suits most people before a meal. Or if you prefer, you can simply serve a bottle of the wine you plan to drink at dinner. (What to drink with the meal, and some basic guidance on choosing and serving wine, is given on page 87.) If you do have spirits, gin, say, with tonic or bitter lemon, and perhaps Scotch – if you are feeling affluent – are perfectly adequate. I think that a vast and complicated array of fancy aperitifs and mixers is both unnecessary and expensive, but on some occasions a specially prepared cup or punch goes down very well. I have had a lot of success with a long cool fruit juice punch in hot summer weather and a mulled (heated up) spiced cup in mid-winter, when guests arrived shivering and glad of something warm.

After dinner make sure the coffee is ready to go, and is real coffee, not instant, however classy the jar. Make your coffee the way you usually make it, but a little stronger for after dinner. If you're not in the habit of making real coffee at all, try coffee bags as a simple, mess-free way of serving your guests. Use half as many coffee bags again as they recommend to get that extra strength and flavour that is so special after a good meal. Serve your coffee in small cups with brown sugar and cream available if you can manage it. With it, serve bitter or dark chocolate, or some kind of sweetmeat. (I know very few people, even those who 'never eat sweets' or who are 'on a strict diet' who will refuse to succumb to those thin, square, chocolate-covered mints.) I usually serve the coffee away from the dining table, in the living room, and have some not-too-expensive cigars and some cigarettes for my friends who smoke.

On the vexed question of smoking in general, your own habits are going to have to decide much of your policy. I do think, however, if you have spent a lot of time preparing delicious food it is reasonable to discourage people from smoking while they are actually eating it, and for that reason I don't provide ashtrays until the meal is over.

If you're going to serve a drink after dinner, brandy is traditional, with perhaps also a flavoured liqueur. However, I find more and more people these days prefer the slightly lighter effect of a glass of good, old port, whether ruby or tawny. Whatever else, make sure your coffee pot is as near to the legendary bottomless condition as possible, because it's amazing how much coffee can be drunk while the conversation is going, and everyone is having a good time.

Saying 'Goodnight'

I usually find that the only parties that have gone on too long are those which feel like it's 3.00 a.m. when it's still before midnight. It's only force of circumstances that ever makes me leave or stop an evening I am really enjoying. If, however, you are stuck with a guest or guests who don't know when it is time to say goodnight – don't plump up their cushions or ask if the baby-sitter might be getting nervous. My favourite ploy is to offer to go and make 'just a last cup of coffee' implying you are sure they are about to leave but would like to delay them just a little longer in order to offer them one last piece of hospitality. I have never known it to fail as it manages to combine a compliment – *ie* the desire to continue in their company – with the inevitability of their immediately pending departure. If it doesn't work – *then* try plumping up the cushions; if your guests are that thick-skinned they probably won't notice.

BASIC RULES FOR A SUCCESSFUL DINNER PARTY

Eat away from the kitchen.

Get everything ready on the table as far in advance as you can – cold dishes ready on the table are fine if they will survive out of the fridge.

Keep the table setting simple but pretty.

Use sideboards and side tables for all the difficult bits and to have as much to hand as possible.

Have enough light to see by, but not so much as to reveal all.

Remember *especially* – the idea is that you and your guests enjoy yourselves – no rule is worth following if it is going to stop that happening.

Buffets-and Some Informal Occasions

Buffets are usually pretty large affairs, whether they're grand and impressive or simply for fun. My own preference for buffets is to have between twelve and twenty people, but the size of your house or flat is going to have to dictate that. Better to have it a little crowded than too empty. It's the one sort of party when you can afford to mix a lot of people who otherwise might never have come into contact with each other. The size of the group and the presentation style of the food means that they can mingle easily, chatter away, make friends or split up and find other people to talk to without offence or effort. It's a good way to get people together for some purpose, whether it's a public one, like organizing a committee or celebrating the first night of the amateur operatic society, or a more subtle plan like match-making between a couple of friends. If the latter's your idea, buffet parties are ideal. There are far too many people present for anyone to be suspicious of your motives. A little judicious introducing should give them as much help as they need, or indeed ought to get (it's no fun unless they do some of it for themselves).

But a buffet can also be a grand way of saying 'thank you' or 'congratulations' to a group of people, or to an individual. And while buffets can be expensive lavish affairs, they can be one of the cheapest ways of entertaining there is. On page 84 you will find a posh version for forty guests followed by a cheap and cheerful meal for twenty.

There are a few general rules to follow, whether it's a simple or sophisticated spread. First, *make sure you've got enough real crockery and cutlery* to manage the number of people you're having. Paper plates won't do! Nor will plastic forks or paper cups. Borrow from a neighbour if you have to, hire them, talk to a local restaurant, but make sure you've got enough. Even for informal entertaining, I really do think proper plates are a necessity. I am not one of those people who believe 'finger foods' a good idea. It may have been all right for Henry VIII, when the floor was covered in rushes and there was a large fireplace to toss the bones in and large dogs to eat them if you missed. For me, at best, it means greasy fingers with nowhere to wipe them and, at worst, a handful of something I really don't want to eat, with nowhere to put it down. Finger food reaches its lowest point at the cocktail party, that most appalling form of entertainment known to western man. If it's nice, it keeps passing you by on the way to somebody else and you can't have seconds. If it's not nice, there's usually not even an ashtray nearby to put the remains in. All in all then, I'm really pretty solidly in favour of plates, whatever the occasion.

Don't underestimate the amount of food that your guests are capable of demolishing. Buffet parties can be very more-ish, with people coming back and helping themselves to things they like. So make sure that you have got enough food to cope with that eventuality. If you aren't used to estimating quantities for a lot of people, the table opposite will give you some basic guidance as to the amount to allow when serving soup, say, or coffee. If there's a dish you know is especially popular, try and make sure you've got a second line of defence with further supplies waiting in the kitchen.

When you arrange the room and set out the table, think about what can best be described as 'traffic flow'. Where are people coming from? Where are they going to go to when they've got their plates full? What order are they going to want to put the food on the plates? *Try and build a logical sequence:* plate, food, seasonings, sauces, chutneys, knife, fork, spoon; and somewhere separate, the glasses and drinks, whatever they are. If you can persuade somebody else to look after these while you look after the food, it makes for much greater peace of mind. Do try to have somewhere away from the serving table where people can sit, once they have helped themselves to what they fancy. There will usually be some who positively can't manage without a table, so make sure there is one, other than the serving table, for your guests to sit at should they wish to do so.

Quick guide to party quantities

Food	Makes 12 portions	Makes 20 portions	Practical points
Soup	2·3 litres (4 pints)	3·4 litres (6 pints)	If made ahead, refrigerated and reheated, cream soups may need thinning with stock
Rice	550 g (1¼ lb) uncooked	900 g (2 lb) uncooked	Cook ahead and reheat in boiling water for 5 minutes
French dressing	300 ml (½ pint)	400–600 ml (¾–1 pint)	Make in a lidded container and shake together just before serving
Meat (with bone) (boneless)	1·8 kg (4 lb) 1·4 kg (3 lb)	3·2 kg (7 lb) 2·3 kg (5 lb)	For buffets: cold cuts, barbecues, cutlets, casseroles, meatballs etc
Poultry (turkey) (chicken)	3·6-kg (8-lb) oven-ready bird 3-kg (6½ lb) oven-ready bird	6·4-kg (14-lb) oven-ready bird 2 2·7-kg (2 6-lb) oven-ready birds	For cold platters with stuffing added
Delicatessen: ham, tongue, salami etc	1·1 kg (2½ lb)	1·8–2·3 kg (4–5 lb)	For a cold platter
Pâté	900 g (2 lb)	1·4–1·8 kg (3–4 lb)	As an appetiser or to include in a buffet selection
Ice cream	2 family size blocks	2·3 litres (4 pints)	Keep at ice cube compartment temperature for easy serving
Cream (single or double)	900 ml (1½ pints)	1·1 litres (2 pints)	To lighten and extend well chilled double cream, add 15 ml (1 tbsp) milk to each 142-ml (5-fl oz) carton cream before whipping. 142 ml (5 fl oz) cream, whipped, gives about 12 individual whirls
Coffee (ground)	150 g (5 oz) coffee; 1·7 litres (3 pints) water; 900 ml (1½ pints) milk; 225 g (8 oz) sugar	250–275 g (9–10 oz) coffee; 3·4 litres (6 pints) water; 1·7 litres (3 pints) milk; 450 g (1 lb) sugar	If you make the coffee in advance, strain it after infusion. Reheat without boiling. Serve hot milk and sugar separately

If you've got a really special occasion to cater for, like a wedding anniversary or an engagement party, a centrepiece on the table is a marvellous idea. But remember, whatever you use to decorate the table, whether it's a wedding cake, a great bowl of fruit or a board piled high with regional cheeses, after 25 or 30 people have been helping themselves it is going to need to be a pretty robust arrangement to still look appetising and attractive.

For an event like a wedding reception, where guests are likely to arrive all at the same time, organization is really essential. You need to have plates, cutlery and glasses already laid out, so people can collect all they need, help themselves to the food and move on to find somewhere to sit and enjoy it.

Finally, you'll make the occasion a lot easier for yourself – or your helpers – if you equip yourself with a nice big tray for the used plates.

Spontaneous parties

Then there's the casual kind of party, when friends just drop in, the round-the-fire, eating-on-the-knee kind of evening. I've quite strong views about this sort of occasion. Firstly, if you are going to entertain people in front of the telly or on the floor listening to records, make sure you know them very well. They can drop sauce on your carpet or kick a wine glass across the parquet, stand up to cheer their team in Match of the Day (forgetting they've got a plate on their knees), or just turn out to disagree with your opinion on the news or taste in music. You're going to need to know them very well indeed to make sure the evening's a success!

This kind of party is usually spontaneous, and there's not a lot you can do in the way of planning. In the room where you eat, though, there are still one or two points worth noting. An occasional or coffee table to actually put the food on is a good idea, even if people haven't got enough room to get their plates on it while they eat. It keeps the food up off the floor, which is both more hygienic and less conducive to it being kicked, knocked over or even trodden on. It will probably make it look a little nicer as well. Use a tray to bring as much in as you can, not forgetting seasonings, chutneys and sauces. Don't bother with things like side plates. One plate to keep balanced on your knee is quite enough. A big communal dish for bread and butter is best.

As to the food itself, keep it simple, preferably eatable just with a fork, and not requiring a lot of complicated serving or accompaniments. Breakfast-type food is often good for this sort of party; omelettes, say, or scrambled eggs. The Eggs Florentine recipe that's listed as a starter (page 44) can be produced in large quantities and makes a smashing on-the-knee TV snack. Soup's not a good idea, but casseroles without too much liquid are suitable. My favourite food of this type is an Italian dish called Pasta carbonara. You make a sauce out of eggs beaten together, mix a little salami or anchovies into the pasta and while it is still piping hot pour over the sauce so that the eggs scramble gently in the heat of the dish without any other cooking. Sprinkled with cheese and served immediately, it takes quite a lot of beating. For quantities, you need to allow 2 eggs and 100 g (4 oz) salami to each 225 g (8 oz) uncooked weight of pasta.

Another favourite dish of mine in this context is the super Spanish omelette that's listed in the main course section (page 38). Easy to do, and it can be adapted to anything you happen to have left in the fridge, if it's an unexpected piece of entertaining you're involved in.

Good bread and butter is a valuable addition to this kind of meal, as you can mop up the plate afterwards with it, as well as providing the bulk that potatoes or rice might have added.

For pudding, to follow any of these main dishes, fruit and cheese is the best – and also the least messy – answer.

Sunday lunch

Sunday lunch is one of my favourite kinds of informal eating. It has all sorts of advantages. You usually have enough time to do the shopping and cook without a panic. It means that families and friends can get together without the worry about baby-sitters, or getting home in time, or missing last buses. It means that children (if you've got them) can come and take part, enchant their grandparents, or learn to become part of the social scene, depending on how old they are. The traditional Sunday lunch recipes, if you like them, work fine for gatherings like that, but seem to me to be both a lot of hard work and extremely expensive. The cost of a joint of roast beef large enough to feed eight or ten people makes your eyes water all through the meal, and could quite take away the pleasure of the company. What I favour is a large filling casserole with some kind of simple starch – potatoes in their jackets, rice, or pasta pieces – and a vegetable appropriate to the time of year, cooked in the winter, salady in the summer.

To follow, a plate of one or two good cheeses served in generous quantities, and lots of fresh fruit that can be eaten with the cheese or on its own. A huge bunch of grapes, overflowing the dish, hanging over the sides, looks incredibly luxurious and doesn't always break the bank. Crusty French bread, lots of butter, and someone to help with the washing-up make this sort of meal the ideal one to entertain at the weekend. Don't be tempted to try for fancy puds or complicated starters, unless you really want to spend the whole time in the kitchen. Almost any of the casserole dishes in the book would fit the pattern. I have a soft spot for one of the rich beef recipes myself.

Picnics with Style

There's a very big difference between eating out of doors – Picnics, and cooking out of doors – Barbecues (more on these, by the way, on page 80). Barbecue food essentially can be eaten anywhere, it just needs usually to be *cooked* outside because of the fumes from the charcoal. I'm not saying that it isn't best eaten outside, where the fresh air seems to add a whet to the appetite, but picnic food just has to be eaten outside. Or at least sitting in the car looking outside if it is actually pouring with rain of course.

I think picnics are really of two kinds. The classic French 'Dejeuner sur l'herbe' where the meal is the object of the exercise, and the outdoors is just a sunny, natural setting; and the English type where the food is really a means of sustaining life in a place whose beauty, position or facilities make one want to be (where the hamburger stands haven't yet reached). Of the two, I tend to favour the former although the latter has its virtues in certain circumstances – being hungry is the principal one of these.

I do like picnics, they're fun, and there's a sense of adventure in getting one together and setting out on it. I think the best single piece of advice is the one the great Escoffier used about cooking in general – 'fait simple' – in other words, don't overdo it. Even sophisticated meals out of doors shouldn't be fussy.

Déjeuner sur l'herbe

A picnic is one of those rare occasions when finger food has its place. Something to start with that can be picked up, wandered about with, canoodled if not canoed over, is ideal. A main course that is rich and filling, and a pudding that *is* a pudding but doesn't make too much fuss about it, is the ideal pattern for me. So too is a real table cloth, real plates, knives and forks, real glasses, and real ice for the drinks. I do draw the line at real napkins, but the other things are what makes the difference between a casual gobble and one of the luxuries of life. There's a quality of pleasure in seeing a snowy white cloth spread on the grass, with places set out on it and delicious food in the middle, that has few equals for me. And if the sun happens to be shining, and the birds chirping, that's an added bonus.

The failure of the sun to shine in a guaranteed manner is one of the reasons, by the way, why I suggest a warm main course (there's a Pasta ragout recipe that's ideal at the end of this section). If you're in the South of France preparing the meal, a giant salad with tuna and peppers, anchovies and hard-boiled eggs will probably be a better alternative. For our British climate, though, why not try starting with slices of brown bread with their crusts cut off, buttered, sprinkled with some chopped walnuts, seasoned and rolled round an asparagus spear (canned or frozen not only will do, but is probably a better bet), like a mini Swiss roll. The combination of bread, asparagus and crunchy nuts is terrific, so make plenty of the rolls and maybe have a small bowl of mayonnaise to dip the ends in as they are eaten.

The English picnic

For the English style picnic you'll forgive me if I'm a little Irish and suggest a French loaf. If sardine or pilchard sandwiches and an eating apple are your style when tramping over hill and moor, that's fine. For me, however fine the view and remote the spot, something a little more in keeping with the aesthetic experience I am undergoing is to my taste. I suggest a French loaf because it makes a really super kind of sandwich. Split it in half lengthwise, scoop out a little of the crumb (you can use it for breadcrumbs in other things), butter it thoroughly, both top and bottom, and it's ready to be filled with one of a variety of fillings. Choose your own favourite, but amongst mine are: fresh tomatoes with a can of anchovies, oil and all, spread amongst them, seasoned with a little home-made lemon French dressing, basil, salt and pepper. The sharpness of the anchovies, and sweetness of the tomatoes combine marvellously.

Or, try a layer of lettuce leaves, flaked canned

tuna, mayonnaise and some radish slices to give the whole thing a bit of a crisp crunch.

Sliced hard-boiled eggs and slices of creamy Mozzarella-type cheese and tomatoes alternating, with a little herb salad dressing is another smashing alternative.

Perhaps my favourite is slices of cooked chicken, very thin pieces of apple (dipped in lemon juice to stop them going brown), lettuce, mango chutney and mayonnaise – a very gooey and extremely delicious combination. Keep the loaf whole until you get it to the picnic site. Take a sharp knife, and slice it diagonally into 5–7·5-cm (2–3-in) sections. You'll be amazed at how fast what looked like a long loaf will disappear into quite ordinary looking people. I usually like, especially in view of our weather, to have a flask of hot soup with me. Any flavour will do. The quick Tomato and orange soup in the starter section (see page 46) is one of the best travellers.

I am also a great believer in a few hard-boiled eggs, not so much as a standby but as an integral part of this kind of picnic. And a bag of prepared crudités, sticks of washed celery, carrots peeled and halved lengthways, cos lettuce leaves washed and shaken dry, also adds a little freshness and crunch if you're using a sandwich filling that tends to be soft and slurpy.

Take along some sweet plain biscuits and some dark or bitter chocolate. A perfect combination that Elizabeth David once suggested and I think has rarely been surpassed.

Whatever kind of picnic you're going on, don't forget that the open air really does sharpen up people's appetites, and it makes them very thirsty too. Generous quantities are very important and so, in my experience, is something to sustain the troops about two or three hours after the real picnic is finished. Just what to take is up to you and your individual taste, but I have been known to be lionised for being able to produce a small rich fruit cake and a large flask of hot tea by the time we were back at the car. I have even known occasions when those two items appeared to be the only protection we had against total melancholy caused by the howling gale raging just the other side of the windscreen. It's a nice comforting feeling knowing it's sitting there waiting for you. And after all, comfortable feelings are part of what being crafty is about.

Here's the recipe for the hot main course I suggested earlier, together with one for a delicious and equally portable pudding to follow.

PASTA RAGOUT

900 g (2 lb) boned shoulder of lamb
45 ml (3 tbsp) vegetable oil
450 g (1 lb) onions, skinned and chopped
396-g (14-oz) can Italian tomatoes
5 ml (1 level tsp) garlic salt
5 ml (1 level tsp) dried oregano
salt and freshly ground pepper
225 g (8 oz) shell or corkscrew pasta pieces
30 ml (2 tbsp) undiluted orange squash

Cut the meat into 2·5-cm (1-in) cubes. Fry it in the oil until it's browned all over. Put in a casserole. Add the onion to the fat, fry and toss for 2 minutes until lightly coated. Add that to the casserole plus all the other ingredients except the pasta and squash. Add enough water for the meat to be generously covered. Simmer on top of the stove with the lid on until the meat is tender, about 1½ hours. Add the pasta and orange squash. Season, stir and cook for another 10 minutes.

At this point you can load the car and depart to the picnic site, covering the casserole with two layers of aluminium foil, and tying the lid on TIGHT, so that spillages can't occur. Just wrap the casserole in a few sheets of newspaper, put it in a cardboard box and into the boot of the car. Not only will it stay hot, the pasta will finish cooking, and the whole will be deliciously savoury, ready to eat up to an hour and a half afterwards. Chunks of French bread are perfect with this, and a salad to follow. *Serves 4–6*

PICNIC PUDDING

two 20-cm (8-in) sponge cakes, made or
  bought
411-g (14½-oz) can pear halves in syrup
4 chocolate flake bars, crumbled
90 ml (6 level tbsp) raspberry jam

Put one of the cakes in a dish large enough to hold it securely. Sprinkle about 90 ml (6 tbsp) of the syrup from the pears over the cake. Slice all but two of the pear halves and place evenly over the cake. Sprinkle with two of the crumbled flake bars, place the second cake on top and spread with raspberry jam. Cut the remaining pear halves neatly in half, arrange them around the cake and sprinkle with remaining flake bars. This confection will travel remarkably well when things with whipped cream come apart, and the pears, chocolate and raspberry flavours combined are unusual and delicious. *Serves 6–8*

Thirty Main Courses

Here is a choice of thirty main courses for your party, whether it is a dinner or a lunch, and at the foot of each are a couple of suggestions for starters and puddings that I think will suit it. You've therefore got a choice of menus based on each main course. If you think something else will go much better, try it – mine are *only* suggestions. I have also indicated where appropriate the sort of vegetables you might like to serve with it (some more ideas for vegetables and other accompaniments will be found at the end of this chapter). The menus are planned so that there won't be too much last-minute work in the kitchen or too many dishes involving fiddly preparation on the same occasion.

Another unusual feature throughout the recipe file is that there are two columns of quantities, so by doubling either the left hand column, for four people, or the right hand column, for six, you arrive at the quantities to use for eight people, or (if you're foolhardy enough) twelve people respectively. For ten people you simply add the left and right columns together.

Most books on entertaining tell you to try dishes out on your family first, and that is certainly not a bad idea – if you have got the time and the money. If you are limited for both, however, I hope you will find most of these – if not foolproof – at least pretty difficult to get so badly wrong that you cannot get away with it with a cool presentation and a lot of confidence. If you do have a disaster, check with Rescue Operations at the back of the book – but don't let on and they'll probably never know the difference.

SHRIMPS NEW ORLEANS

In Louisiana, they have shrimps the size of our baby lobsters, but even our smaller cousins can come up trumps in the spicy sauce from the Queen of Southern Cities!

Serves 4		Serves 6
1	clove of garlic, skinned and chopped	1
30 ml (2 tbsp)	vegetable oil	45 ml (3 tbsp)
1 medium	Spanish onion, skinned and chopped	1 large
1 medium	red pepper, seeded and chopped	1 large
1 medium	green pepper, seeded and chopped	1 large
226-g (8-oz)	can tomatoes	396-g (14-oz)
	salt and freshly ground pepper	
2·5 ml ($\frac{1}{2}$ level tsp)	allspice	3·75 ml ($\frac{3}{4}$ level tsp)
2·5 ml ($\frac{1}{2}$ level tsp)	cayenne pepper	3·75 ml ($\frac{3}{4}$ level tsp)
450 g (1 lb)	shrimps, peeled (the *bigger* the better)	700 g ($1\frac{1}{2}$ lb)

Fry the chopped garlic in the oil for 1 minute, then add the chopped onion and peppers. Fry for 5 minutes, then add the tomatoes and their juice. Cook for 15 minutes. Season, add the spices and shrimps and cook for just 5 minutes – they can get rubbery if you do them much longer.

Serve with boiled rice and a salad afterwards.

Suggested starters and desserts

Chicken liver pâté (page 41) Cinnamon pears (page 62)
Potted cheese (page 43) Bananas Foster (page 69)

MEDITERRANEAN FISH CASSEROLE

Rich, aromatic and spicy – this dish is not for the timid! It's not difficult to cook, but should really be kept for your special friends: those whose happiest memories are of a little candlelit taverna on some sunkissed Greek isle, where the scent of lemons wafts on the breeze and the scent of garlic on the kitchen steam.

Serves 4		Serves 6
225 g (8 oz)	onions, skinned	350 g (12 oz)
3	cloves of garlic, skinned and crushed	4
60 ml (4 tbsp)	vegetable oil	90 ml (6 tbsp)
396-g (14-oz)	can tomatoes	800-g (28-oz)
450 g (1 lb)	squid – small for choice	700 g (1½ lb)
450 g (1 lb)	coley, skinned	700 g (1½ lb)
600 ml (1 pint)	mussels, scrubbed and bearded	600 ml (1 pint)
2·5 ml (½ level tsp)	chilli powder	3·75 ml (¾ level tsp)
5 ml (1 level tsp)	dried basil	7·5 ml (1½ level tsp)
5 ml (1 level tsp)	dried oregano	7·5 ml (1½ level tsp)
	salt and freshly ground pepper	
100 g (4 oz)	prawns, peeled	175 g (6 oz)

Chop the onion finely and fry with the garlic in oil for 5 minutes until golden. Add the tomatoes and simmer, covered, for 15 minutes. Stir until smooth. Clean the squid; wash under a tap – the purple skin just peels off. Take out all the insides and discard (including the transparent quill). You can keep the tentacles, but pull out the hard 'beak' in the middle. Cut the squid into rings, and the coley into 2·5-cm (1-in) cubes and add them with the mussels to the sauce. Add the chilli, herbs and seasoning and simmer for just 5 minutes. Add the prawns and simmer for 1 minute more.

Serve with rice or – best of all – crusty bread.

Suggested starters and desserts

Roman-style artichokes (page 42) Queen's pudding (page 67)
Cold cucumber soup (page 50) Pancakes with grapes and honey (page 67)

RICH FISH PIE

For too many of us fish pie is a horror story from school. If that's so in your family, this version should correct any nightmarish memories. The only problem with it is that you really need a second one waiting in the oven after they've demolished the first round. Try it; it'll keep very well in the freezer if their eyes turn out to be bigger than their tummies.

Serves 4		Serves 6
450 g (1 lb)	cod, coley or whiting fillet	700 g (1½ lb)
300 ml (½ pint)	water and milk	400 ml (¾ pint)
1 medium	onion, skinned and chopped	1 large
30 ml (2 level tbsp)	flour	45 ml (3 level tbsp)
25 g (1 oz)	butter	40 g (1½ oz)
100 g (4 oz)	button mushrooms	175 g (6 oz)
100-g (4-oz)	packet frozen mixed vegetables	100-g (4-oz)
100 g (4 oz)	shrimps, peeled	175 g (6 oz)
2	hard-boiled eggs, quartered	3
450 g (1 lb)	warm mashed potato	700 g (1½ lb)
1	egg, beaten	1

Poach the fish in the liquid with the onion for about 8 minutes. Take out and flake into big pieces. Make a sauce with the flour, whisking it together with the butter and the liquid that the fish was cooked in. Add the mushrooms – washed not peeled – and mixed vegetables and simmer for 2 minutes. Mix in the fish and shrimps. Put into a pie dish and add the quartered eggs. Cover with mashed potato, brush with beaten egg and bake for 25 minutes at 190°C (375°F) mark 5.

Suggested starters and desserts

Leeks provençale (page 47)
Tomato and orange soup (page 46)
Baked codlings (page 64)
Fancy fruit salad (page 71)

SOLE VÉRONIQUE

Fish and grapes may seem a bit outlandish at first, but not only is this one of the classic sole dishes, it's not that surprising really – remember our own mackerel and gooseberries. Absolutely delicious! Give it a try – you'll be surprised by the balance of flavours.

Serves 4		Serves 6
	2 soles, filleted and skinned (lemon okay, Dover are best) 3	
	salt and freshly ground pepper	
300 ml ($\frac{1}{2}$ pint)	white grape juice	400 ml ($\frac{3}{4}$ pint)
	juice of 1 lemon	
150 ml ($\frac{1}{4}$ pint)	double cream	200 ml (7 fl oz)
5 ml (1 level tsp)	flour	10 ml (2 level tsp)
7 g ($\frac{1}{4}$ oz)	butter	15 g ($\frac{1}{2}$ oz)
100 g (4 oz)	white grapes, halved and seeded	175 g (6 oz)

Put the sole fillets in a baking dish, season and cover with the grape and lemon juice. Bake at 190°C (375°F) mark 5 for 15 minutes until the fish is just done. Strain the juice into a pan and add the cream. Whisk in the flour and butter and then whisk the mixture over heat until thick and smooth; season. Place the grape halves along the fillets, pour the sauce over and heat in the oven for 5 minutes.

Serve with new potatoes and a green salad.

Suggested starters and desserts

Stuffed tomatoes (page 43)
Ratatouille (page 45)
Ginger ice cream (page 62)
St Clement's syllabub (page 66)

MONK FISH ALMONDINE

Monk fish is one of the great crafty secrets. In France and Italy it's treated as a luxury but here, although it reminds me of lobster, it's cheaper than cod. Pester your fishmonger.

Serves 4		Serves 6
700 g (1½ lb)	monk fish fillets	1 kg (2¼ lb)
300 ml (½ pint)	apple juice	400 ml (¾ pint)
1	bay leaf	1
150 ml (¼ pint)	single cream	225 ml (8 fl oz)
25 g (1 oz)	butter	40 g (1½ oz)
15 ml (1 level tbsp)	flour	30 ml (2 level tbsp)
50 g (2 oz)	ground almonds	75 g (3 oz)
15 ml (1 tbsp)	lemon juice	20 ml (4 tsp)
75 g (3 oz)	grated cheese (preferably Gruyère)	100 g (4 oz)
5 ml (1 level tsp)	salt	7·5 ml (1½ level tsp)
	freshly ground black pepper	

Put the fish in a shallow oval dish. Pour the juice over and bake with the bay leaf for 20 minutes at 180°C (350°F) mark 4. Drain and keep the fish warm. Whisk the juices with the cream, butter and flour over heat until it thickens. Add the almonds, lemon juice, cheese, and seasoning; stir and pour over the fish.

Put under the grill until the top is brown and bubbly, and serve with mashed potatoes and broccoli or beans.

Suggested starters and desserts

Spinach salad with mushrooms (page 44) St Clement's syllabub (page 66)
Roman-style artichokes (page 42) Granita lemone (page 60)

BAKED LAMB ROMAN-STYLE

In Rome, where this dish comes from, they use lamb so young that a leg will only just about feed two people. With our rather larger joints a lamb shoulder will feed four and you and your guests should find this dish rich and very tender. Ask your butcher to cut the joint into four or six pieces.

Serves 4		Serves 6
1 medium	onion, skinned and finely chopped	1 large
15 ml (1 tbsp)	vegetable oil	15 ml (1 tbsp)
15 ml (1 tbsp)	vinegar *or* lemon juice	30 ml (2 tbsp)
5 ml (1 level tsp)	dried sage	7·5 ml (1½ level tsp)
2·5 ml (½ level tsp)	dried rosemary	3·75 ml (¾ level tsp)
60 ml (4 level tbsp)	tomato paste	90 ml (6 level tbsp)
5 ml (1 level tsp)	garlic salt	7·5 ml (1½ level tsp)
2·5 ml (½ level tsp)	pepper	3·75 ml (¾ level tsp)
1·4-kg (3-lb)	shoulder of lamb on the bone, trimmed	2-kg (4½-lb)

Fry the onion in the oil until soft. Mix the other ingredients in a bowl, add the onion and use to coat the lamb pieces. Bake in a covered casserole at 170°C (325°F) mark 3 for 1 hour, or until the lamb nearly falls off the bone. Remove protruding bones and skim off the excess fat before serving.

Serve with long green beans and new or sauté potatoes.

Suggested starters and desserts

Cold cucumber soup (page 50) Ice cream with strawberry sauce (page 64)
Avocado salad (page 46) Coffee cream cheese (page 62)

MILANESE LAMB CUTLETS

A crisp lemony coating and tender moist meat make an unusual way of eating that perennial favourite, lamb chops. A dish to cook when you're in a hurry but still want to impress.

Serves 4		Serves 6
8	best end of neck cutlets – chined (this is with only the long bone left on them)	12
1	egg, beaten	1
75 g (3 oz)	breadcrumbs – a packet is fine	100 g (4 oz)
30 ml (2 level tbsp)	grated lemon rind	45 ml (3 level tbsp)
150 ml ($\frac{1}{4}$ pint)	vegetable oil	150 ml ($\frac{1}{4}$ pint)
25 g (1 oz)	butter	25 g (1 oz)

Dip the cutlets in the beaten egg and then the breadcrumbs and lemon rind mixed. (A paper bag to shake them in is a good idea.) Fry them in the oil and butter until golden on both sides – about 8 minutes a side.

Serve with sauté potatoes (or chips) and courgettes sliced and cooked in a little butter with the lid on for 5 minutes.

Suggested starters and desserts

Spinach salad with mushrooms (page 44)
Tagliatelle with tuna sauce (page 52)
Chocolate chestnut mould (page 72)
Berry cream sponge (page 73)

CHICKEN WITH ROSEMARY

This is a nice easy recipe for a summer evening – or serve on winter nights to bring back memories of summer with the sharp Mediterranean smell of rosemary. Fresh rosemary is best, but dried is okay.

Serves 4		Serves 6
30 ml (2 level tbsp)	flour	45 ml (3 level tbsp)
4	chicken portions, skinned	6
30 ml (2 tbsp)	vegetable oil	45 ml (3 tbsp)
300 ml ($\frac{1}{2}$ pint)	chicken stock	400 ml ($\frac{3}{4}$ pint)
60 ml (4 tbsp)	lemon juice	90 ml (6 tbsp)
5 ml (1 level tsp)	dried rosemary	7·5 ml (1$\frac{1}{2}$ level tsp)
5 ml (1 level tsp)	salt	7·5 ml (1$\frac{1}{2}$ level tsp)

Flour the chicken and fry gently for 10 minutes in oil in a frying pan. When golden, just cover with the stock and mix in the lemon juice. Add the rosemary and salt. Simmer for 20 minutes, so the sauce thickens. Taste, and season if necessary.

Serve with courgettes and shell pasta.

Suggested starters and desserts

Salad with shrimps (page 49)
Stuffed tomatoes (page 43)
Pears belle Hélène (page 59)
Pancakes with grapes and honey (page 67)

LIVER VENETIAN STYLE

This dish, the Venetian version of our more prosaic liver and onions, needs a little trust to try it, as its cooking methods are hardly orthodox. Nevertheless, it's one of the most delicious ways of cooking liver.

Serves 4		Serves 6
2 medium	onions, skinned and thinly sliced	3 medium
15 ml (1 tbsp)	vegetable oil	15 ml (1 tbsp)
30 ml (2 tbsp)	chopped parsley (fresh or dried)	45 ml (3 tbsp)
90 ml (6 tbsp)	water	150 ml ($\frac{1}{4}$ pint)
15 ml (1 tbsp)	cider *or* wine vinegar	30 ml (2 tbsp)
450 g (1 lb)	lambs' liver, very thinly sliced	700 g (1$\frac{1}{2}$ lb)

In a wide pan, fry the onions for 5 minutes in the oil until soft but not brown. Add the parsley, water and vinegar and bring to the boil. Add the liver and cook it quickly, turning once, for about 2–3 minutes only.

Serve the liver with the onions on top and with rice mixed with green peas. (Called risi and bisi in Venice.)

Suggested starters and desserts

Shrimps with melon (page 52) Cinnamon pears (page 62)
Crab tart (page 54) Ananas sauvage (page 65)

SPICED CHICKEN WITH PEPPERS

This is a dish with more than a hint of spice and a feeling of the hot Mediterranean summer about it. If you're looking for something just a little different to do with the perennial chicken, this is it.

Serves 4		Serves 6
4	chicken portions	6
15 ml (1 tbsp)	vegetable oil	30 ml (2 tbsp)
25 g (1 oz)	butter	25 g (1 oz)
2 medium	red or green peppers, seeded and sliced	3 medium
2 medium	onions, skinned and sliced	3 medium
5 ml (1 level tsp)	garlic salt	5 ml (1 level tsp)
226-g (8-oz)	can tomatoes	396-g (14-oz)
	pinch each of basil and oregano	
	generous pinch of chilli powder	

Fry the chicken portions in the oil and butter until they are golden (about 10 minutes). Add the pepper and onion to the chicken and fry, adding after 5 minutes the garlic salt, canned tomatoes, herbs and chilli powder. If it looks dry add a little water. Simmer for 25 minutes.

Serve with rice and green beans.

Suggested starters and desserts

Sardines or sprats doré (page 42)
Avocado salad (page 46)
Orange fool (page 63)
Pears belle Hélène (page 59)

CLUBMAN'S KIDNEYS

As well as a lot of strange traditions like refusing ladies membership, the gentlemen's clubs of Pall Mall were renowned for their very fine cooking. This rich, very simple dish, which was developed in clubland, is in that tradition of masculine cooking that women can at last share.

Serves 4		Serves 6
12	lamb kidneys	18
75 g (3 oz)	butter	75 g (3 oz)
15 ml (1 level tbsp)	prepared mustard	20 ml (4 level tsp)
30 ml (2 tbsp)	Worcestershire sauce	45 ml (3 tbsp)
60 ml (4 tbsp)	tomato sauce	90 ml (6 tbsp)
30 ml (2 level tbsp)	chutney – mango is nicest	45 ml (3 level tbsp)
300 ml ($\frac{1}{2}$ pint)	beef stock	400 ml ($\frac{3}{4}$ pint)

Clean, skin and split the kidneys in half and remove the cores. Fry gently in the butter for 5 minutes. Add the mustard, sauces and chutney and stir for 1 minute. Raise the heat and add the stock. Stir and simmer for a further 5 minutes.

Serve with mashed potatoes, carrots and parsnips.

Suggested starters and desserts

Potted cheese (page 43)   Royal cream (page 60)
Crab tart (page 54)   French apple pudding (page 66)

SOUTHERN FRIED CHICKEN

This is the recipe that reveals Colonel Sanders' secret. Southern-style fried chicken is very different because of the steam pressure cooking it gets towards the end. Give 'em a taste of this and they'll all be singing Dixie!

Serves 4		Serves 6
4	chicken portions	6
45 ml (3 level tbsp)	flour	75 ml (5 level tbsp)
15 ml (1 level tbsp)	ground cinnamon	20 ml (4 level tsp)
5 ml (1 level tsp)	garlic salt	7·5 ml (1$\frac{1}{2}$ level tsp)
1	egg, beaten	1
600 ml (1 pint)	vegetable oil	600 ml (1 pint)
300 ml ($\frac{1}{2}$ pint)	milk	400 ml ($\frac{3}{4}$ pint)

Cut each chicken portion into 2 pieces and dust them with the flour mixed with cinnamon and garlic salt. Dip each piece in beaten egg and coat again with the cinnamon flour mixture. Heat about 0·5–1 cm ($\frac{1}{4}$–$\frac{1}{2}$ in) oil in a wide frying pan. (Most people think that Southern fried chicken is deep fried, but it is not.) When the oil is hot, fry the chicken quickly on both sides to seal it, then – and this is the secret of Southern fried chicken – cover the pan. This will make the chicken crisp on the outside and steamed on the inside. Cook for 15 minutes, leaving the lid off for the last 5 minutes to crisp it up well.

To make the gravy, pour almost all the oil out of the pan, add the surplus cinnamon flour and fry for 1 minute. Stir in the milk, bring to the boil and cook for 2–3 minutes: this will make a thick creamy-coloured gravy.

Mashed potatoes, sweetcorn and fried bananas are the traditional accompaniments.

Suggested starters and desserts

Caesar salad (page 46)   Chocolate gâteau (page 68)
Pumpkin and leek soup (page 51)   Marmalade ice cream (page 74)

STEAK WITH MUSTARD AND ORANGE

An unusual combination of flavours makes this steak recipe a firm favourite. Do try and find the real grainy, French-style mustard, even if it's made in England – as much of it is these days. Traditional English mustard just doesn't add up to the same flavour.

Serves 4		Serves 6
four 225-g (8-oz)	rump *or* entrecôte steaks	six 225-g (8-oz)
5 ml (1 tsp)	vegetable oil	10 ml (2 tsp)
300 ml ($\frac{1}{2}$ pint)	orange juice	400 ml ($\frac{3}{4}$ pint)
5 ml (1 tsp)	Worcestershire sauce	10 ml (2 tsp)
50 g (2 oz)	butter	50 g (2 oz)
60 ml (4 level tbsp)	grainy French mustard	90 ml (6 level tbsp)

Heat a frying pan big enough for the steaks, until it is very hot. Brush with oil and sear the steaks for 1 minute on each side. Add the orange juice, Worcestershire sauce and butter; heat for 5 minutes. Remove the steaks, add the mustard and stir for 1 minute. Pour the sauce over the steaks and season.

Serve immediately, with sauté potatoes and red cabbage.

Suggested starters and desserts

Salmon pâté (page 51)
French country vegetable soup (page 58)
Mont Blanc (page 69)
Blackberry cobbler (page 63)

NAVARIN PRINTANIER

Spring lamb stew is the proper translation of this dish, but I think you'll find that it's pretty good at any time of the year. The important thing is not to add the vegetables until the meat is nearly done so the whole lot is just coming to the point of perfection at the same time.

Serves 4		Serves 6
700 g (1$\frac{1}{2}$ lb)	fillet of lamb	1 kg (2$\frac{1}{4}$ lb)
30 ml (2 level tbsp)	flour	45 ml (3 level tbsp)
15 ml (1 tbsp)	vegetable oil	20 ml (4 tsp)
225 g (8 oz)	button onions, skinned	350 g (12 oz)
600 ml (1 pint)	beef stock	900 ml (1$\frac{1}{2}$ pints)
225 g (8 oz)	new carrots, scraped	350 g (12 oz)
225 g (8 oz)	new potatoes, washed not peeled	350 g (12 oz)
5 ml (1 level tsp)	salt	7·5 ml (1$\frac{1}{2}$ level tsp)
	freshly ground pepper	
225 g (8 oz)	button mushrooms	350 g (12 oz)
7 g ($\frac{1}{4}$ oz)	butter, melted	15 g ($\frac{1}{2}$ oz)
15 ml (1 level tbsp)	tomato paste	30 ml (2 level tbsp)

Cut the meat into small neat pieces 1 cm ($\frac{1}{2}$ in) across. Dust them with flour and fry them in oil in a sauté pan for 10 minutes, stirring gently. Add the onions and stock and bring to the boil – turn down and simmer for 10 minutes. Add the carrots, potatoes and seasoning; cover and simmer until the potatoes are cooked (about 15 minutes). Toss the button mushrooms in the melted butter and add them with the tomato paste – heat through for 1 minute.

Serve with crusty French bread and a salad to follow.

Suggested starters and desserts

Avocado salad (page 46)
Eggs in aspic (page 56)
Pancakes with cheese and lemon (page 67)
Berry cream sponge (page 73)

MEDITERRANEAN CHICKEN

This is a dish that is perfect for a lazy type of day, when it can be savoured at leisure, carrying you back with memories of the villages of Southern France where it originated.

Serves 4		Serves 6
450 g (1 lb)	potatoes, peeled	700 g (1½ lb)
45 ml (3 tbsp)	vegetable oil	45 ml (3 tbsp)
3	cloves of garlic, skinned and crushed	3
1·4-kg (3-lb)	chicken, skinned	2-kg (4½-lb)
2·5 ml (½ level tsp)	dried tarragon	3·75 ml (¾ level tsp)
2·5 ml (½ level tsp)	dried basil	3·75 ml (¾ level tsp)
	salt and freshly ground pepper	
225 g (8 oz)	tomatoes, skinned and chopped	350 g (12 oz)
	black olives (optional)	

This needs a heavy metal casserole dish. Cut the potatoes into 1-cm (½-in) cubes. Fry them for 10 minutes in 30 ml (2 tbsp) hot oil; take them out. Add the rest of the oil, garlic and whole chicken. Turn until brown, about 10 minutes. Season with the tarragon, basil, salt and pepper. Add the tomatoes, cover and simmer very gently for 40 minutes. Don't let it burn – add a little water if it starts to. When cooked, test the chicken with a skewer – the juices should run clear. Add the potatoes, and black olives if you like them. Take the lid off, raise the heat and stir until the potatoes are properly cooked – about 10 minutes.

Serve with a tossed green salad.

Suggested starters and desserts

Kippers Michelin (page 55)   Coffee cream cheese (page 62)
Sardines or sprats doré (page 42)   French apple flan (page 74)

SHOULDER OF LAMB IN THE BRETON MANNER

In the French province of Brittany they have some of the best lamb in the world, and this dish was devised specially to show it off. It's one for you to show off with too. A very grand version of roast lamb. No mint sauce with it, though, please. Redcurrant jelly is okay. Even the French don't frown on that. Ask the butcher to cut the surplus fat off the shoulder of lamb – this is important.

Serves 4		Serves 6
3	cloves of garlic, skinned	4
1·4-kg (3-lb)	shoulder of lamb	2-kg (4-lb)
5 ml (1 level tsp)	dried rosemary	10 ml (2 level tsp)
700 g (1½ lb)	stringless green beans, fresh if possible	900 g (2 lb)

Cut the garlic into halves. Prod 6 (8) little holes in the lamb – evenly spaced around it – and insert half a clove of garlic in each hole. Sprinkle the lamb with the rosemary and roast at 180°C (350°F) mark 4, for 1 hour on a rack over a tin. Blanch the beans for 6 minutes (if they are frozen this is not necessary) and place them in the tin under the lamb. Roast for another 20–30 minutes.

Serve the lamb surrounded with the beans – which now have a lovely taste – and new potatoes.

Suggested starters and desserts

Crab tart (page 54)   Mont Blanc (page 69)
Eggs in aspic (page 56)   French apple flan (page 74)

STEAK, SHELLFISH AND MUSHROOM PIE

This dish needs a little planning in advance. For a spectacular occasion, it's normally greeted with all the 'Oohs and ahhs' you could wish. In its original form it was made with oysters – when they cost a pound a barrel. If you're feeling rich you can still use them, but mussels make a more than acceptable substitute.

Serves 4		Serves 6
450 g (1 lb)	stewing steak	700 g (1½ lb)
25 g (1 oz)	butter	40 g (1½ oz)
15 ml (1 level tbsp)	flour	30 ml (2 level tbsp)
1	onion, skinned and chopped	1
100 g (4 oz)	mushrooms	175 g (6 oz)
600 ml (1 pint)	beef stock	600 ml (1 pint)
100 g (4 oz)	mussels, cleaned	175 g (6 oz)
210-g (7½-oz)	packet puff pastry (frozen is best)	369-g (13-oz)

Cut the steak into cubes and fry in the butter for 5 minutes until brown. Sprinkle with the flour and brown again. Add the onion and mushrooms, cover with the stock and simmer for about 2–2½ hours, or until tender. Cook the mussels in boiling salted water for 5 minutes. Remove them from the shells and add them to the steak. Put the mixture into a pie dish. Roll out the pastry and use to cover the dish. Flute the edge of the pastry, then bake at 200°C (400°F) mark 6 for 30–35 minutes.

Serve with boiled potatoes and hot buttered beetroot.

Suggested starters and desserts

Potted cheese (page 43)
Sprouts polonaise (page 50)
Compote of oranges (page 60)
Chocolate chestnut mould (page 72)

DAUBE MACARONIDE

One of the secrets of crafty cooking is not to give yourself too much to do. This casserole can be done in advance, and just heated up on the day you want to eat it. The macaroni shells make an unusual and very simple accompaniment.

Serves 4		Serves 6
900-g (2-lb)	leg of beef	1·4-kg (3-lb)
15 ml (1 tbsp)	vegetable oil	30 ml (2 tbsp)
2 medium	onions, skinned and chopped	3 medium
396-g (14-oz)	can tomatoes	396-g (14-oz)
600 ml (1 pint)	beef stock	900 ml (1½ pints)
5 ml (1 level tsp)	garlic salt	7·5 ml (1½ level tsp)
2	bay leaves	3
5 ml (1 level tsp)	dried thyme	7·5 ml (1½ level tsp)
50 g (2 oz)	black olives, stoned (optional)	75 g (3 oz)

Cut the meat into 5-cm (1-in) cubes; do not throw away the fat and sinew. Fry in the oil until brown – about 5 minutes. Add the onion and fry for 5 more minutes, then add the tomatoes and their juice to the pan with the beef stock. Season with garlic salt, add the bay leaves and thyme; simmer for 2 hours on top of the cooker. If you are using expensive beef it won't need as long, but it is less authentic. The sauce will thicken on its own. Five minutes before serving, remove the bay leaves and add the black olives, if liked.

Serve with macaroni shells or macaroni pieces cooked in the usual way, using some of the sauce from the meat to mix in and moisten them before serving.

A green salad is nice with this.

Suggested starters and desserts

Tomato and orange soup (page 46)   Marmalade ice cream (page 74)
Smoked mackerel pâté (page 55)   Fancy fruit salad (page 71)

CAULIFLOWER LASAGNE

A fabulous crafty and economical variation on one of the classic Italian pasta dishes. If you think it also reminds you of one of Britain's favourites, Cauliflower cheese, you're quite right. The Anglo-Italian combination is almost irresistible. If you can't get 'no-boil' lasagne, ordinary will do, but you have to boil it first.

Serves 4		Serves 6
450 g (1 lb)	minced beef	700 g (1½ lb)
1 medium	onion, skinned and chopped	1 large
1	clove of garlic, skinned and crushed	1
30 ml (2 tbsp)	vegetable oil	45 ml (3 tbsp)
	salt and freshly ground pepper	
396-g (14-oz)	can tomatoes	396-g (14-oz)
10 ml (2 level tsp)	dried basil	15 ml (1 level tbsp)
45 ml (3 level tbsp)	flour	60 ml (4 level tbsp)
900 ml (1½ pints)	milk	1·1 litres (2 pints)
50 g (2 oz)	butter	75 g (3 oz)
175 g (6 oz)	grated cheese	225 g (8 oz)
1 small	cauliflower	1 medium
225 g (8 oz)	lasagne – Barilla *or* Zara 'no-boil'	350 g (12 oz)

Fry the meat, onion and garlic in oil for 5 minutes and season. Add the tomatoes and basil and simmer for 10 minutes. Make a white sauce: mix the flour with a little milk first, add the butter and the rest of the milk, then bring to the boil and whisk gently until it thickens. Add half the cheese and season. Break the cauliflower into small florets. Butter a baking dish and put the cauliflower in an even layer over the bottom, seasoning well. Cover with a third of the cheese sauce, then a layer of lasagne, then half the meat mixture, then a little more cheese sauce – repeat layers, finishing with a layer of lasagne covered with cheese sauce. Sprinkle with the remaining cheese and dot butter over the top if you like. Bake for 45–50 minutes at 180°C (350°F) mark 4.

A green salad is nice with this.

Suggested starters and desserts

Minestrone (page 43)   Compote of oranges (page 60)
Stuffed three delicious (page 57)   Praline ice cream (page 73)

PAELLA
Illustrated on the cover

In Spain every Sunday after dinner, each household washes up its paella pan and hangs it up until the next time. You don't have to wait until Sunday for this dish. And any of your guests with an ounce of 'Olé!' in their souls will be singing 'Granada' in no time at all.

Serves 4		Serves 6
1–1·4-kg (2–3-lb)	chicken	1·8–2·3-kg (4–5-lb)
15 ml (1 tbsp)	olive oil	30 ml (2 tbsp)
1 medium	onion, skinned and chopped	2 medium
225 g (8 oz)	long grain rice	350 g (12 oz)
400 ml ($\frac{3}{4}$ pint)	chicken stock	600 ml (1 pint)
	pinch saffron	
226-g (8-oz)	packet frozen mixed vegetables	340-g (12-oz)
100 g (4 oz)	prawns, peeled	175 g (6 oz)
5 ml (1 level tsp)	garlic salt	7·5 ml (1$\frac{1}{2}$ level tsp)
5 ml (1 level tsp)	paprika	7·5 ml (1$\frac{1}{2}$ level tsp)
50 g (2 oz)	black olives, stoned (optional)	75 g (3 oz)
100 g (4 oz)	mussels, cleaned and cooked (optional)	175 g (6 oz)

Joint the chicken, or use 4 (6) chicken portions and fry them gently in the oil for 15 minutes. Take out. Add the onion and the rice to the oil and stir until coated. Add the chicken stock, which you have dissolved the saffron in, stir into the rice, bring to the boil then turn down to a low simmer. Add the chicken on top and cook until the rice is done – for about 20 minutes. Stir in the mixed vegetables and the peeled prawns and heat for 5 minutes. Season with the garlic salt and paprika, and decorate with black olives and cooked mussels on the half shell if you want to use them.

Serve with a salad, if liked.

Suggested starters and desserts

Stuffed tomatoes (page 43)   Orange fool (page 63)
Guacamole (page 49)   Granita lemone (page 60)

BEEF STROGANOFF

Invented – so they say – for a Russian Prince, who was crazy about soured cream. Beef stroganoff is one of the quickest and easiest dinner dishes I know. It should keep the wolves from the door!

Serves 4		Serves 6
700 g (1$\frac{1}{2}$ lb)	rump *or* sirloin steak	1 kg (2$\frac{1}{4}$ lb)
350 g (12 oz)	Spanish onions, skinned	450 g (1 lb)
225 g (8 oz)	button mushrooms	350 g (12 oz)
50 g (2 oz)	butter	75 g (3 oz)
	salt and freshly ground pepper	
300 ml ($\frac{1}{2}$ pint)	soured cream	300 ml ($\frac{1}{2}$ pint)
15 ml (1 level tbsp)	French mustard	20 ml (4 level tsp)

Slice the meat into 1-cm (½-in) strips across the grain. Slice the onions into 0·5-cm (¼-in) slices. Wash – don't peel – the mushrooms and halve them. Heat the butter until it foams. Add the beef and brown very quickly, then add the onions and mushrooms and toss carefully for 2 minutes. Season, add the cream and mustard and stir until heated through.

Serve immediately on a bed of white rice.

Suggested starters and desserts

Danish soused herrings (page 55)
Eggs and artichokes (page 58)
Praline ice cream (page 73)
Apple pancakes (page 65)

HUNGARIAN GOULASH

Three things always seem to be associated with Hungary. Gypsies, violins and goulash. I don't think any of them are unique to Hungary but they do all seem to have reached their high point in that country. The recipe that follows is not for those who like their food plain, simple and 'not messed about'. It's one of the richest and most delicious stews ever invented. The gypsies and violins are up to you!

Serves 4		Serves 6
900 g (2 lb)	chuck steak, trimmed	1·4 kg (3 lb)
15 ml (1 tbsp)	vegetable oil	15 ml (1 tbsp)
25 g (1 oz)	butter	25 g (1 oz)
1 large	Spanish onion, skinned and chopped	2 large
2	cloves of garlic, skinned and crushed	3
900 ml (1½ pints)	beef *or* chicken stock (cubes will do)	1·1 litres (2 pints)
141-g (5-oz)	can tomato paste	141-g (5-oz)
30 ml (2 level tbsp)	paprika	45 ml (3 level tbsp)
	salt and freshly ground pepper	
15 ml (1 level tbsp)	cornflour	20 ml (4 level tsp)
15 ml (1 tbsp)	water	15 ml (1 tbsp)
150 ml (¼ pint)	soured cream	150 ml (¼ pint)

Cut the meat into 2·5-cm (1-in) cubes, and fry in the oil and butter in a large casserole or frying pan until lightly browned. Add the onion and garlic and turn them until well coated. If you are using a frying pan tip the contents into a casserole, add the stock, tomato paste and paprika; season well and stir thoroughly to ensure the tomato paste and paprika are evenly distributed. Simmer on top, or in the oven at 180°C (350°F) mark 4 for 2 hours, with a lid on.

Blend the cornflour and water together, add to the sauce and simmer again until it has thickened. Serve in bowls with noodles, and put a dollop of soured cream in the middle of each bowl at the last minute. You can add mushrooms or potatoes to the goulash to make it go further. The Hungarians aren't purists in the matter, and nor am I.

Suggested starters and desserts

Kippers Michelin (page 55)   Crème caramel (page 61)
Sprouts polonaise (page 50)   Hot fruit salad (page 72)

CARBONADE OF BEEF

Every country cooks its beef in whatever it has locally. This recipe from Belgium uses lager to make some of the richest gravy there is.

Serves 4		Serves 6
900 g (2 lb)	stewing beef	1·4 kg (3 lb)
50 g (2 oz)	flour	75 g (3 oz)
15 ml (1 tbsp)	vegetable oil	30 ml (2 tbsp)
25 g (1 oz)	butter	25 g (1 oz)
450 g (1 lb)	onions, skinned and sliced	700 g (1½ lb)
300 ml (½ pint)	lager	400 ml (¾ pint)
300 ml (½ pint)	beef stock	400 ml (¾ pint)
	salt and freshly ground pepper	
	bouquet garni	
30 ml (2 tbsp)	chopped parsley	30 ml (2 tbsp)

Cut the meat into pieces roughly half the size of a postcard and 0·5 cm (¼ in) thick. Dust with some of the flour and fry in oil and butter until brown, about 5 minutes, and then transfer to a casserole. Fry the onions in the same oil for 2 minutes. Sprinkle with remaining flour and mix with the beef. Rinse out the hot pan with lager and add with the stock to the beef. Season, add the bouquet garni (herbs in a little muslin bag bought ready prepared) and cook in the oven at 170°C (325°F) mark 3 for 3 hours. Remove the bouquet garni and sprinkle with parsley before serving.

Serve with mashed potatoes, with any vegetables afterwards as a course on their own.

Suggested starters and desserts

Eggs Florentine (page 44)   Strawberry fool (page 69)
Stuffed tomatoes (page 43)   Pancakes palatschinken (page 67)

MEAT BALLS WITH GINGER GRAVY

This is an adaptation of a German dish called Sauerbraten. The Germans make it with the same sort of beef we'd eat with Yorkshire pudding, but this version is both cheap and delicious, capturing some of the very unusual flavours of the original dish. However much you may be surprised at the ingredients, stick with them: you will be delighted with the result.

Serves 4		Serves 6
700 g (1½ lb)	minced beef	1 kg (2¼ lb)
30 ml (2 tbsp)	malt vinegar	45 ml (3 tbsp)
30 ml (2 tbsp)	tomato sauce	45 ml (3 tbsp)
1	egg, beaten	1
5 ml (1 level tsp)	garlic salt	7·5 ml (1½ level tsp)
2·5 ml (½ level tsp)	dried parsley	5 ml (1 level tsp)
2·5 ml (½ level tsp)	dried thyme	5 ml (1 level tsp)
	salt and freshly ground pepper	
15 ml (1 tbsp)	beef dripping *or* oil	25 ml (1½ tbsp)
about 300 ml (½ pint)	beef stock	about 450 ml (¾ pint)
50 g (2 oz)	gingernut biscuits, finely crushed	75 g (3 oz)
15 ml (1 level tbsp)	German or mild English mustard	30 ml (2 level tbsp)

Mix the meat, vinegar, tomato sauce, egg, garlic salt, herbs and seasoning together. Knead until smooth. Make the meat balls about 3·5 cm (1½ in) in diameter. Fry them gently in the beef dripping in a frying pan wide enough to get them all in in one layer. When lightly browned, about 5 minutes, pour in enough beef stock to almost cover them, and simmer gently for 25 minutes. Take out the meat balls, put them in a warm serving dish and add the crushed gingernuts to the liquid in the pan, stirring steadily until you have a smooth purée. Add the mustard and bring to the boil, when it will thicken and darken. If the sauce tastes too sweet, add another 5–10 ml (1–2 tsp) vinegar and bring to the boil again.

Pour over the meat balls and serve with mashed potatoes, and red cabbage cooked slowly with a little sliced onion and grated apple.

It may sound bizarre but it tastes marvellous.

Suggested starters and desserts

Spinach salad with mushrooms (page 44) Cheesecake (page 75)
Guacamole (page 49) Yogurt crunch (page 76)

CHICKEN SIMLA

The flavours of this dish come from our imperial past – the splendours of the Raj, tiffin at the club in Simla. But this recipe, though it has eastern promise, won't sear your oesophagus!

Serves 4		Serves 6
15 ml (1 level tbsp)	curry powder	25 ml (1½ level tbsp)
15 ml (1 level tbsp)	caster sugar	25 ml (1½ level tbsp)
5 ml (1 level tsp)	salt	7·5 ml (1½ level tsp)
4	chicken portions	6
60 ml (4 level tbsp)	mango chutney	90 ml (6 level tbsp)
45 ml (3 tbsp)	Worcestershire sauce	60 ml (4 tbsp)
50 g (2 oz)	butter, melted	75 g (3 oz)
45 ml (3 tbsp)	lemon juice	60 ml (4 tbsp)

Stir the curry powder, caster sugar and salt together and spoon on to the chicken; leave for at least 2 hours. Heat the grill for 5 minutes (preferably lined with foil). Grill the chicken skin side up for 10 minutes – turn and grill for a further 5–8 minutes. Mix all the other ingredients and pour carefully over the chicken. Grill for 10–15 minutes until bubbling gently.

Serve with rice and a green salad and be sure to pour *all* the juices over the chicken.

Suggested starters and desserts

Guacamole (page 49) Mango fool (page 66)
Potted tongue (page 41) Ananas sauvage (page 65)

PIGEON CASSEROLE

This is one of the cheapest and nicest ways of getting the flavour of game, without the trouble of hanging and the other rather dubious paraphernalia that often goes with cooking fur and feathers.

Serves 4		Serves 6
4	pigeons, cleaned	6
15 ml (1 tbsp)	vegetable oil	30 ml (2 tbsp)
25 g (1 oz)	butter	50 g (2 oz)
225 g (8 oz)	button onions, skinned	350 g (12 oz)
	bouquet garni	
300 ml ($\frac{1}{2}$ pint)	apple juice	400 ml ($\frac{3}{4}$ pint)
150 ml ($\frac{1}{4}$ pint)	water	225 ml (8 fl oz)
	salt and freshly ground pepper	
225 g (8 oz)	button mushrooms	350 g (12 oz)
	grated rind and juice of 1 orange	

Turn the pigeons in the hot oil and butter for 5 minutes until browned and then place in a casserole. Brown the onions lightly and add to the pigeons with the bouquet garni. Pour over the apple juice and water to cover, seasoning well. Bake at 180°C (350°F) mark 4 for 1 hour. Add the mushrooms and the orange rind and juice and cook for a further 30 minutes.

Remove the bouquet garni, season and serve with lots of mashed potato – the gravy can be thickened, but it's nice as it is.

Suggested starters and desserts

Piperade (page 48)
Smoked haddock mayonnaise (page 51)
Chocolate gâteau (page 68)
Apple pancakes (page 65)

CHICKEN WITH ASPARAGUS

The French have a name for a boneless piece of chicken cut from the breast. They call it the suprême, and I think that teamed with the royal vegetable asparagus, this is really chicken with class!

Serves 4		Serves 6
4	breasts of chicken, boned	6
25 g (1 oz)	butter	40 g (1$\frac{1}{2}$ oz)
15 ml (1 tbsp)	vegetable oil	15 ml (1 tbsp)
150 ml ($\frac{1}{4}$ pint)	water	225 ml (8 fl oz)
15 ml (1 level tbsp)	flour	25 ml (1$\frac{1}{2}$ level tbsp)
150 ml ($\frac{1}{4}$ pint)	double cream	225 ml (8 fl oz)
226-g (8-oz)	packet frozen asparagus (or a can will do)	226-g (8-oz)
2·5 ml ($\frac{1}{2}$ level tsp)	salt	3·75 ml ($\frac{3}{4}$ level tsp)
	freshly ground pepper	

Fry the chicken in butter and oil for 5 minutes. Add the water to cover and poach gently for about 15 minutes. Take out the chicken and keep warm. Whisk the flour into the liquid and then the cream. Add the asparagus, reserving a little for garnish. Season, heat through until boiling and then serve poured over the chicken pieces. Garnish with the asparagus.

Suggested starters and desserts

Caesar salad (page 46)   Strawberry fool (page 69)
Beef lindstrom (page 54)   Orange fool (page 63)

MINT GLAZED LAMB CHOPS

Lamb and mint are age-old favourites, but this quickie dish brings a different dimension to the honourable association. Serve with mashed potatoes and new peas for the classic accompaniments.

Serves 4		Serves 6
4–8	loin or chump chops	6–12
15 ml (1 tbsp)	vegetable oil	30 ml (2 tbsp)
15 ml (1 level tbsp)	garlic salt	20 ml (4 level tsp)
60 ml (4 level tbsp)	mint jelly	90 ml (6 level tbsp)

Heat the grill for 10 minutes at maximum. Brush the chops with oil and grill for 4 minutes. Turn over and season with garlic salt. Spread the jelly on the meat and grill for another 5 minutes. Before serving, spoon any drippings back over the meat – delicious!

Suggested starters and desserts

Quick green pea soup (page 57)   French apple pudding (page 66)
Smoked salmon scramble (page 56)   Chocolate mousse (page 75)

DUCK WITH CHERRIES

Perhaps one of the grandest dinner party dishes of all. This duck is rich, golden and crisp – the sweet and sour quality of the cherries sets the flavour off beautifully.

Serves 4		Serves 6
1·8-kg (4-lb)	oven-ready duck, defrosted if necessary	2·3–2·6-kg (5–6-lb)
425-g (15-oz)	can morello cherries	425-g (15-oz)
10 ml (2 level tsp)	arrowroot	10 ml (2 level tsp)
	salt and freshly ground pepper	

Pour 600 ml (1 pint) of boiling water over the duck in a colander. Let it dry and then roast it in the oven at 200°C (400°F) mark 6 for 20 minutes to the 450 g (1 lb). Make sure the duck is on a rack over the roasting pan to let the fat come out. When the duck is golden brown, remove from the pan and keep warm. Add 30 ml (2 tbsp) of the drippings to the cherries, plus the arrowroot mixed in a little water. Bring the mixture to the boil until it thickens and clears, then season and serve with the duck.

Serve with creamed potatoes and a salad afterwards.

Suggested starters and desserts

Noodles à la crème (page 45)
Smoked mackerel pâté (page 55)
Pavlova (page 70)
Royal cream (page 60)

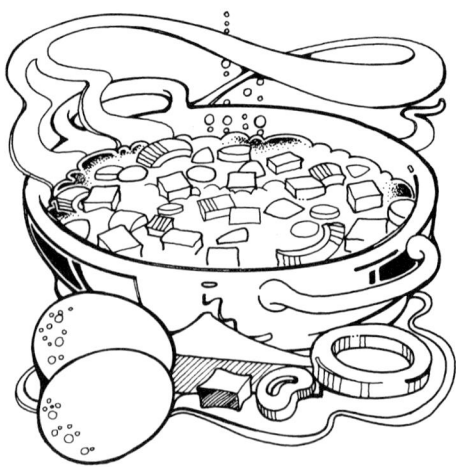

SPANISH OMELETTE

This is the great standby dish of all time. It can be made with whatever you have, and looks bright and cheerful as well as tasting delicious. Any of the ingredients can be replaced by a substitute, except the eggs and onions – you can use shrimps for salami, mushrooms instead of cheese, etc.

Serves 4		Serves 6
60 ml (4 tbsp)	oil – olive is best	90 ml (6 tbsp)
1 medium	onion, skinned and chopped	2 medium
226-g (8-oz)	packet frozen mixed vegetables	226-g (8-oz)
225 g (8 oz)	cooked potatoes, diced	350 g (12 oz)
100 g (4 oz)	salami, cubed	175 g (6 oz)
8	eggs, beaten	12
	salt and freshly ground pepper	
100 g (4 oz)	cheese, cubed	175 g (6 oz)
	fresh or dried herbs	

Heat the oil in a large frying pan and fry the onion for 3 minutes. Add the mixed vegetables – still frozen – and the potato and fry for another 3 minutes. Add the salami and eggs beaten with the seasoning. Mix together thoroughly, then let the omelette set over a low heat. Add the cheese cubes and sprinkle with fresh or dried herbs.

Serve from the pan cut in wedges like cake, with hot crusty bread chunks and a green salad to make it a meal to remember.

Suggested starters and desserts

Gazpacho (page 53)   Caramel oranges (page 63)
Sardines or sprats doré (page 42) French apple flan (page 74)

. . . And Some Accompaniments

Almost all the main dishes in this book need one prime addition and that is an accompanying form of starch as well as a green vegetable or salad. It's quite strange, but people somehow don't feel they've had a proper meal unless there's something solid and ribsticking to go with what they are eating, and to soak up the delicious juices and gravy that are on their plates.

Around the world, if you think about it, the kind of food people eat is really defined by the starch base they eat with it. The Chinese are thought of as rice eaters, the Irish as potato eaters, the Italians as pasta eaters. In this country we are very lucky, because although potatoes do loom large in the British tradition, we also have a tradition of bread, rice, even these days of pasta. So what follows are a few crafty ways of cooking them, both labour and time saving – and also a few ideas for some unusual and delicious vegetable dishes to go with your dinner.

Potatoes

If they are young or new potatoes, do *not* peel them. Wash them carefully, boil them in their skins, toss them in a little butter, and garlic salt if it is suitable to the dish it is to accompany, and some freshly ground black pepper. Most of the flavour is in the skin and if they are washed and cooked, they look delicate and marbled – not grotty and dirty.

If the potatoes are older or you want something a little more substantial; wash them and slice them, still unpeeled, into 0·5-cm ($\frac{1}{4}$-in) rounds, put them in flat layers in a deep casserole with a knob of butter and a little salt and pepper between each layer. Add enough milk to come to within 2·5 cm (1 in) of the top of the potatoes. Bake for about $1\frac{1}{4}$ hours at 190°C (375°F) mark 5; the milk will all be absorbed into the potatoes which will be tender and have a lovely brown crusty top.

In the winter try baking big floury potatoes which make a wonderful accompaniment to most stews, casseroles and dishes with a lot of gravy. Just wash them and rub with a little oil before baking for about 1 hour at 180°C (350°F) mark 4.

Rice

To begin with, you must buy long grain rice. The best kind of all is called Basmati, or there is another kind called Patna. You can find most of them in good shops or supermarkets, or in an Indian or Oriental shop if you've got one near you. Don't buy pre-fluffed rice or any of the pre-packaged ones, unless you really feel you'd only be happy or successful with them. They are easier to cook but have little flavour and not as much nourishment as the more natural kind.

To cook rice, bring a large saucepan of water to the boil, add a pinch of salt and 5 ml (1 tsp) of oil. Wash the rice under a little running hot water (unless it's pre-fluffed) until the water runs clear. Tip it into the boiling water and leave it to cook for 9–12 minutes, testing it carefully to make sure that it doesn't overcook and go soggy. When the rice is perfectly cooked you should just be able to squeeze a grain through with your thumb and forefinger without too much problem. When it is cooked, turn it into a sieve, not a colander, and run another saucepanful of hot water through it. This separates the grains which you can then keep in a warm covered bowl or saucepan for up to half an hour without it coming to any harm.

Pasta

To serve with main dishes, try the very short-cut, twisted, macaroni-like 'corkscrew' variety, or one of the medium-sized pasta 'shell' varieties. To cook, try a new method recently developed in Italy, which provides a much greater degree of safety for the inexperienced pasta cook in getting it to the right texture.

To a large saucepan of boiling water, add 10 ml (2 level tsp) salt and 5 ml (1 tsp) oil. Add the pasta carefully and keep at a rolling boil for 3 minutes exactly. Switch off, cover and leave for 7–10 minutes, depending on how thick the pasta was originally. It will cook completely through in that time and just needs draining, tossing with a little butter or oil and serving. You can leave it in the water for up to 5 minutes after it is cooked, without it deteriorating too much. Pasta cooked like this is smashing for casseroles or rich stews, because it absorbs the flavour of the gravy so splendidly – that's why the Italians use pasta with rich sauces like Bolognese.

Crafty blanched vegetables

The French have a way of cooking vegetables which is to blanch them first, let them cool and then re-heat them in a little butter. A lot of our frozen vegetables have had the blanching process done already, so with a little care, you can produce French-style vegetables from a packet which has just been taken out of the freezer, without anyone knowing. The most suitable vegetables for this, I think, are long green beans and Brussels sprouts – although it does work successfully with frozen peas if you add a little chopped onion.

Take out the frozen vegetables of your choice *while they are still frozen!* Melt a knob of butter in a frying pan. When it is fairly hot – but not browning – add the frozen vegetables and turn them completely so that the butter coats them. It will congeal on the vegetables and look quite extraordinary – don't panic! Continue to cook the vegetables over a moderate heat, turning them thoroughly until they are sizzling in the butter. At this point, turn the heat right down and leave them for a couple of minutes to cook a little more. A lid helps but is not essential. Fresh sea salt and ground black pepper complete the transformation.

A few almonds added to the butter before cooking either sprouts or beans, and a little chopped onion with peas helps a lot too. A small amount of thick cream stirred into the peas transforms them into the delicious accompaniment, Petits Pois à la Francaise – one of the great classics of the French kitchen.

Salads – and salad dressings
The other almost instant vegetable dish of course that goes with so many main courses is a salad. I think you can be a lot more adventurous with what you put into a salad than most people dare. Sliced oranges, chicory and watercress is one combination I love. Green beans, sweet red peppers and pasta shells cooked in the manner described above and left to get cold, is another. What is most important is the dressing, whether it is a lettuce on its own or a more fanciful mixture you are serving. Two dressings which are my favourites are a French dressing made with lemon juice, and a mayonnaise made very easily in a blender as follows:

LEMON FRENCH DRESSING
½ cup of oil
¼ cup of lemon juice
5 ml (1 level tsp) each of salt and French mustard
10 ml (2 level tsp) sugar

Whisk, mix or blend the ingredients thoroughly together and leave to stand for at least 30 minutes before using. The lemon flavour with the oil (which can be olive but is probably better for you if it is sunflower) produces a salad dressing with a lightness of taste that goes with most dishes, where vinegar in the dressing would destroy the flavour of the other parts of the meal.

BLENDER MAYONNAISE
For this you *do* need a blender, but it makes a mayonnaise far superior in many ways than the classic French one that's made with egg yolks and olive oil, which is often too heavy for my taste.

Into the blender goblet put one egg, 5 ml (1 level tsp) of salt, sugar and dry mustard (less mustard if you like milder mayonnaise) and 10 ml (2 tsp) lemon juice. Blend until mixed. Add 30 ml (2 tbsp) oil, blend again and then add gradually – using the drip slot if your blender has one – approximately another 150 ml (¼ pint) oil. (This will vary slightly depending on the size of the egg and its age.) When the mayonnaise is ready, the blender should suddenly slow down its speed and start 'hiccoughing' indicating that the mayonnaise has suddenly become thick. At that point switch it off and take it out of the blender. It will thicken over the next 10 minutes even more than it has done already. It should be of a lovely light consistency and a pale gold in colour.

With s a s, never dress them until the last minute. By all means prepare the vegetables, but make sure they are dry, put them back in the fridge and wait until just before serving to dress them – this applies whether you are using my mayonnaise or Hellmann's, Lemon French dressing or one of the excellent proprietary brands available in most supermarkets.

Forty Simple Soups and Starters

CHICKEN LIVER PÂTÉ

This is a recipe that really does need the blender, unless you're prepared to put in an awful lot of work. The result, however, is one of the richest and most delicious liver pâtés I know. It has the really authentic savour of a mixture created deep in the heart of France, which is where this recipe came from.

Serves 4		Serves 6
225 g (8 oz)	chicken livers	350 g (12 oz)
100 g (4 oz)	butter	175 g (6 oz)
1	clove of garlic, skinned and chopped	1
1	egg, beaten	1
2·5 ml ($\frac{1}{2}$ level tsp)	dried thyme	3·75 ml ($\frac{3}{4}$ level tsp)
pinch	mixed spice	pinch
	salt and freshly ground pepper	

Fry the chicken livers gently in half the butter. When they are still pink inside add the garlic and the egg. Stir until the egg is almost set, then transfer the whole mixture to the blender, with the thyme, mixed spice, seasoning and remaining butter. Blend until smooth.

POTTED TONGUE

An old English favourite, this is a kind of Anglicised pâté. You can make it really quickly with ingredients you can find in almost any supermarket or grocer's, yet it comes out tasting special.

Serves 4		Serves 6
225 g (8 oz)	cooked ox tongue	350 g (12 oz)
175 g (6 oz)	butter	250 g (9 oz)
pinch	cayenne pepper	pinch
pinch	ground mace	pinch
	salt and freshly ground pepper	
50 g (2 oz)	melted butter to finish	75 g (3 oz)

Mash the tongue with a fork in a bowl. Melt the butter and pour all but the dregs over the tongue. Mix thoroughly, season with the spices and salt and pepper and spoon into pretty individual pots. (You can put it all in the blender.) Pour a little melted butter over the top of each pot to seal.

Chill for at least 2 hours and serve with lots of thin brown toast.

SARDINES OR SPRATS DORÉ

This dish is adapted from one of the most famous Provencale ways of dealing with sardines. All along the coast from Marseilles to St. Trop, lunchtime or evening, the sizzle and crunch of the local sardines enlivens every restaurant table. If you can't get sardines, our own small sprats make an admirable substitute.

Serves 4		Serves 6
450 g (1 lb)	sardines *or* small sprats	700 g (1½ lb)
60 ml (4 level tbsp)	flour	90 ml (6 level tbsp)
5 ml (1 level tsp)	salt	7·5 ml (1½ level tsp)
5 ml (1 level tsp)	paprika	7·5 ml (1½ level tsp)
	lemon wedges	

Don't clean the fish, just wash them. Mix together the flour, salt and paprika and roll the fish in it. Fry them in batches of about 10, either in deep fat for 2 minutes, or shallow fat for about 1 minute each side (they occasionally pop). Do not let them get more than golden brown.

Pile them up on a dish surrounded with lemon wedges and serve with French bread and butter. You can serve tartare sauce with them, but it is not really necessary.

The French usually eat the whole fish, but you can leave the heads!

ROMAN-STYLE ARTICHOKES

A recipe for rather a grand dinner party starter. The secret is to get the centre of the artichokes out cleanly, leaving only the fleshy leaves and the rich delicious heart to be covered with the creamy dressing.

Serves 4		Serves 6
4	globe artichokes	6
30 ml (2 tbsp)	lemon juice	45 ml (3 tbsp)
30 ml (2 tbsp)	vegetable oil	45 ml (3 tbsp)
10 ml (2 level tsp)	caster sugar	15 ml (1 level tbsp)
5 ml (1 tsp)	chopped fresh mint	10 ml (2 tsp)
2·5 ml (½ level tsp)	garlic salt	5 ml (1 level tsp)
225 ml (8 fl oz)	mayonnaise (see page 40)	400 ml (¾ pint)

Trim the stalks and pointed tips of the leaves off the artichokes and boil for 20 minutes. Carefully remove the fuzzy centres (under the leaves which join in the centre). Make *sure* you get the bit like tangled cotton out! Drain upside down in a colander and then cool. Stir the lemon juice, oil, sugar, mint and garlic salt into the mayonnaise.

Put the artichokes upright on pretty plates and carefully fill the centres equally with the mayonnaise mixture.

To eat, pull off the outside leaves, dip in the dressing and chew off the fleshy base. The centre that's left after all the leaves are eaten is the heart – and a great delicacy.

MINESTRONE

An almost instant soup which comes out of cans and the freezer, or your refrigerator; only your guests and family will never know. Serve it with no apologies in a white china bowl, with lots of hot crusty Italian-style bread to mop up the last drops of this delicious soup.

Serves 4		Serves 6
226-g (8-oz)	can tomatoes	396-g (14-oz)
283-g (10-oz)	can white haricot beans	283-g (10-oz)
226-g (8-oz)	packet frozen mixed vegetables	340-g (12-oz)
1 medium	onion, skinned and chopped	2 medium
600 ml (1 pint)	beef stock	900 ml (1½ pints)
	salt and freshly ground pepper	
60 ml (4 level tbsp)	grated Parmesan cheese	90 ml (6 level tbsp)

Mix the tomatoes, beans, mixed vegetables and onion together with the stock. Simmer for 10 minutes.

Season and serve with the Parmesan cheese and a look of innocence.

STUFFED TOMATOES

Make this simple dish in the summer and autumn when large tomatoes are plentiful and cheap. It's quite surprising how delicious and fresh-tasting the tomatoes are even when cooked.

Serves 4		Serves 6
8	large tomatoes	12
50 g (2 oz)	fresh white breadcrumbs	75 g (3 oz)
5 ml (1 level tsp)	garlic salt	7·5 ml (1½ level tsp)
1–2	spring onions, trimmed and chopped	2–3
50 g (2 oz)	chicken livers, chopped	75 g (3 oz)
15 g (½ oz)	butter	25 g (1 oz)
30 ml (2 tbsp)	chopped parsley	45 ml (3 tbsp)

Cut the tomatoes in half across the middle (horizontally) and scoop out the pulp. Mix together the breadcrumbs, garlic salt and onion. Fry the liver in the butter for 1 minute. Add the breadcrumb mixture to the frying pan and fry for 2 minutes. Add the tomato pulp and fry for another 2 minutes. Fill the tomatoes with this mixture and bake in the oven at 200°C (400°F) mark 6 for 15 minutes.

Sprinkle with chopped parsley and serve hot.

POTTED CHEESE

The very ordinariness of the ingredients makes even more surprising the piquancy and creamy texture of this special spread – usually a great hit with the gentlemen.

Serves 4		Serves 6
100 g (4 oz)	Cheddar or Double Gloucester cheese, grated	175 g (6 oz)
50 g (2 oz)	butter, melted	75 g (3 oz)
15 ml (1 tbsp)	lemon juice	20 ml (4 tsp)
2·5 ml (½ level tsp)	ground mace	3·75 ml (¾ level tsp)
2·5 ml (½ level tsp)	prepared mustard	3·75 ml (¾ level tsp)

Mash all the ingredients together thoroughly and pack into a little soufflé dish. Melt a little butter to pour on top to seal it.

A little mango chutney in it isn't authentic – but very tangy! Try about 10 ml (2 tsp).
Serve with brown toast.

SPINACH SALAD WITH MUSHROOMS

One of the great classic salads of America, a country where salad has moved to the centre of the culinary stage instead of hovering in the wings. Unusual though the ingredients are in this one, do try it: you and your guests will be more than pleasantly surprised.

Serves 4		Serves 6
450 g (1 lb)	spinach, carefully washed	700 g (1½ lb)
100 g (4 oz)	button mushrooms, washed and sliced	175 g (6 oz)
	For the dressing	
200 ml (7 fl oz)	vegetable oil	300 ml (½ pint)
100 ml (4 fl oz)	lemon juice	150 ml (¼ pint)
5 ml (1 tsp)	clear honey	10 ml (2 tsp)
pinch	salt	pinch

Strip the spinach from its stalks and tear into large bite-size pieces. Put them into a salad bowl. Add the button mushrooms. (Do not peel the mushrooms – crafty cooks just wash them thoroughly.) Whisk the dressing ingredients together, pour over the spinach, toss and serve quickly.

EGGS FLORENTINE

Creamy eggs, rich spinach and a smooth cheesy sauce all come direct from one of the most sumptuous cuisines in the whole of Italy. This is a starter to serve with a little Vivaldi in the background and your best Botticelli on the wall behind you. But even the Beatles and a British Airways calendar won't detract from the taste.

Serves 4		Serves 6
4	eggs	6
450 g (1 lb)	spinach, fresh or frozen	700 g (1½ lb)
25 g (1 oz)	butter	40 g (1½ oz)
	salt and freshly ground pepper	
	ground nutmeg	
60 ml (4 level tbsp)	grated Parmesan cheese	90 ml (6 level tbsp)
	For the sauce	
30 ml (2 level tbsp)	flour	45 ml (3 level tbsp)
568 ml (1 pint)	milk	850 ml (1½ pints)
50 g (2 oz)	butter	75 g (3 oz)

Boil the eggs for exactly 5 minutes. Put in cold water. Shell carefully – the yolks are still soft. Wash the spinach, if fresh, and fry in the butter until soft and dryish. Make a sauce with the flour, milk and butter – mix the flour with a little of the milk, put it with the butter and the rest of the milk in a saucepan and bring to the boil, whisking gently until it thickens.

Mix half the sauce with the cooked spinach and put into a flattish baking dish. Season well and sprinkle with nutmeg. Place the eggs on the spinach and cover with the rest of the sauce and the Parmesan cheese. Put under the grill for 2 minutes only, until sizzling. Serve immediately. Wholemeal bread is nice for scraping the plates.

NOODLES À LA CRÈME

A very good friend of mine who developed this recipe from a classic north Italian dish always serves it at his special dinner parties, calling it 'Springtime, Summer, Autumn or Winter in Tuscany' depending on the season. I suggest you do the same. But don't tell 'em where you got the idea!

Serves 4		Serves 6
225 g (8 oz)	ribbon noodles or tagliatelle	350 g (12 oz)
1	egg	1
150 ml ($\frac{1}{4}$ pint)	double cream	225 ml (8 fl oz)
	salt and freshly ground pepper	
60 ml (4 level tbsp)	grated Parmesan cheese	90 ml (6 level tbsp)

Cook the noodles in boiling salted water for 3 minutes. Leave for 7 minutes with the lid on, away from the heat, then rinse quickly. Beat the egg with the cream, mix with the noodles in a warm bowl, add salt and pepper, sprinkle Parmesan cheese over and eat them quickly while still hot.

Cubes of salami and/or freshly cooked green peas are sometimes added. A few flaked almonds, though not traditional, are also delicious.

RATATOUILLE

Perhaps the most famous of all the vegetable dishes to come out of France. The secret with this one is not to cook the vegetables too long so that they retain their individual flavours and textures while blending into a delicious whole. For close friends try adding a little extra garlic.

Serves 4		Serves 6
225 g (8 oz)	aubergines, trimmed	350 g (12 oz)
225 g (8 oz)	courgettes, trimmed	350 g (12 oz)
225 g (8 oz)	red *or* green peppers, seeded	350 g (12 oz)
225 g (8 oz)	onions, skinned	350 g (12 oz)
1	clove of garlic, skinned and chopped	2
90 ml (6 tbsp)	vegetable oil	120 ml (8 tbsp)
396-g (14-oz)	can tomatoes, drained	396-g (14-oz)
	salt and freshly ground pepper	

Slice all the fresh vegetables thinly. Fry the garlic in the oil for 1 minute and add the fresh vegetables. Turn in oil for 5 minutes. Add the tomatoes *without* the juice — fry gently for 30 minutes, without a lid, turning occasionally. Season highly.

Serve with hot crusty French bread.

CAESAR SALAD

Despite its Roman name, this is another American salad. A mixture of crisp-fried bread cubes, garlic, Parmesan, lettuce and dressing, may seem a little unusual at first, but the combination of textures and the freshness and sharpness of the flavours make this starter a talking point at any dinner party.

Serves 4		Serves 6
1	cos lettuce	1 large
50 g (2 oz)	fried croûtons	75 g (3 oz)
	garlic salt	
60 ml (4 level tbsp)	grated Parmesan cheese	90 ml (6 level tbsp)
	For the dressing	
1	egg	1
100 ml (4 fl oz)	vegetable oil	100 ml (4 fl oz)
45 ml (3 tbsp)	lemon juice	45 ml (3 tbsp)
2·5 ml (½ level tsp)	salt	2·5 ml (½ level tsp)
5 ml (1 level tsp)	sugar	5 ml (1 level tsp)

Wash, dry and tear the lettuce into chunks. Mix these with the croûtons in a bowl. Put the egg in boiling water for 1 minute, break into a bowl, add the dressing ingredients, then beat until creamy.

Pour the dressing over the salad and mix it all up. Shake a little garlic salt and the Parmesan cheese over the salad.

Eat immediately!

TOMATO AND ORANGE SOUP

This is one of the really sneaky recipes that you can have in your larder ready to go whenever you need it. It also tastes surprisingly good hot or cold, and serves as a perfect standby in summer or winter.

Serves 4		Serves 6
600 ml (1 pint)	tomato juice	900 ml (1½ pints)
400 ml (¾ pint)	orange juice	600 ml (1 pint)
1	onion, skinned and finely chopped	1
50 g (2 oz)	butter	50 g (2 oz)
5 ml (1 level tsp)	garlic salt	5 ml (1 level tsp)
	freshly ground pepper	
15 ml (1 tbsp)	chopped parsley, fresh or dried	15 ml (1 tbsp)

Mix the tomato and orange juices and bring them slowly to the boil. In a separate pan, fry the onion in the butter and season with the garlic salt. Tip the mixture into the orange and tomato juice just before it comes to the boil, and simmer for 10 minutes. Serve as it is, after adjusting the seasoning, or liquidise for smooth soup. Sprinkle with parsley. If served cold, some natural or mandarin flavoured yogurt – a spoonful in each bowl – is delicious.

AVOCADO SALAD

The slightly sweet and sour tasting sauce gives a perfect spike to the creaminess of the avocados and the flavour of the shrimps.

Serves 4		Serves 6
100 g (4 oz)	shrimps, peeled	175 g (6 oz)
100 g (4 oz)	pineapple cubes	175 g (6 oz)
60 ml (4 tbsp)	mayonnaise	90 ml (6 tbsp)
15 ml (1 tbsp)	soy sauce	20 ml (4 tsp)
30 ml (2 tbsp)	pineapple syrup	45 ml (3 tbsp)
2	ripe avocados	3

Mix the shrimps and pineapple cubes (if the cubes are too big, cut them into quarters). Stir the mayonnaise, soy sauce and syrup together and add the shrimp mixture. Halve the avocados, remove the stones and pile the shrimp mixture into the cavities.

Chill for 10 minutes and serve.

LEEKS PROVENÇALE

A most unlikely combination of flavours; but one that works remarkably well. For this idea, I am indebted to Elizabeth David, as all of us who enjoy continental cooking in this country so often are. It's delicious hot or cold. I think my preference is for it cold. It will keep in the refrigerator for two or three days if you cover it; a great advantage.

Serves 4		Serves 6
700 g (1½ lb)	leeks	900 g (2 lb)
45 ml (3 tbsp)	vegetable oil	60 ml (4 tbsp)
226-g (8-oz)	can tomatoes	396-g (14-oz)
	grated rind and juice of 1 lemon	
5 ml (1 level tsp)	sugar	7·5 ml (1½ level tsp)
5 ml (1 level tsp)	dried basil	7·5 ml (1½ level tsp)
5 ml (1 level tsp)	dried oregano	7·5 ml (1½ level tsp)
5 ml (1 level tsp)	garlic salt	7·5 ml (1½ level tsp)

Trim the leeks, cutting off the *straggly* green bits, and cut into 10-cm (4-in) lengths. Clean the white part of the leeks very carefully leaving them as whole as possible. Heat the oil and fry the leeks like sausages, rolling them for 3 minutes. Add the tomatoes and half their juice, the juice of the lemon and the sugar – simmer covered for 15–20 minutes. Add the herbs, the garlic salt and the lemon rind. Turn up the heat and stir for 1 minute.

Serve hot with French bread and butter, or let them get cold and eat as a starter.

BROWN RICE SALAD

This is one to experiment with, and perhaps to offer your vegetarian friends. But even meat eaters like the combination of nutty rice and crunchy bits with a sharp lemony dressing. Made in sufficient quantity it can also be the basis for a summer barbecue salad. Although you can eat this dish hot or cold, I must admit I prefer it cold.

Serves 4		Serves 6
225 g (8 oz)	brown rice	350 g (12 oz)
1	cucumber, deseeded and diced	1
4	sticks of celery, chopped	6
8	radishes, sliced	12

optional additions are pineapple cubes; diced
eating apple; shelled walnuts; cooked frozen vegetables

For the dressing

30 ml (2 tbsp)	lemon juice	45 ml (3 tbsp)
60 ml (4 tbsp)	salad oil	90 ml (6 tbsp)
5 ml (1 level tsp)	brown sugar	7·5 ml (1½ level tsp)
5 ml (1 level tsp)	garlic salt	7·5 ml (1½ level tsp)
5 ml (1 level tsp)	prepared mustard	7·5 ml (1½ level tsp)

Cook the rice in boiling salted water for about 30 minutes; it needs stirring occasionally and should be cooked covered if possible. Whisk all the dressing ingredients together in a bowl. When the rice is just tender, which takes 30–40 minutes depending on the rice, drain it carefully, rinse it in hot water and dress it with the dressing. Do this while the rice is still warm. Let it cool and mix in the chopped vegetables, and any of the additional flavourings you like. Let the flavours blend for at least 30 minutes and serve it as a first course or as a main course with other salads.

PIPERADE

From the borders of France and Spain where the Basques live, comes one of the nicest and simplest of starters. Don't let the eggs get too hard. It'll still taste okay but the texture won't make the same creamy sauce for the crisp, bright vegetables. It can be eaten cold, too.

Serves 4		Serves 6
1 medium	onion, skinned and sliced	1 large
1 medium	red pepper, seeded and sliced	1 large
1 medium	green pepper, seeded and sliced	1 large
60 ml (4 tbsp)	oil (olive is ideal)	90 ml (6 tbsp)
4	fresh tomatoes, skinned and sliced	6
6	eggs	9
	salt and freshly ground pepper	
2·5 ml ($\frac{1}{2}$ level tsp)	paprika	5 ml (1 level tsp)

Fry the onion and peppers in the oil for 5 minutes in a big frying pan. Add the sliced tomatoes and cook for another 5 minutes. Break the eggs and stir them into this mixture, without beating first. Season with salt, pepper and paprika – (remember *not* chilli pepper). Stir until creamy but not hard.

Serve while hot, with hot French bread.

SALAD WITH SHRIMPS

If you ever thought shrimp cocktail was good news, just wait until you try this version with one of my favourite dressings. Even without the shrimps it's pretty good; with them a totally new experience. This is a one dish meal that I love serving at lunchtime at a weekend.

Serves 4		Serves 6
1	crisp lettuce (Webb's Wonderful is best)	1 large
1 bunch	radishes, trimmed and sliced	1 bunch
1 bunch	spring onions, trimmed and chopped	1 bunch
100 g (4 oz)	shrimps, peeled	175 g (6 oz)
	For the dressing	
200 ml (7 fl oz)	salad oil	300 ml ($\frac{1}{2}$ pint)
100 ml (4 fl oz)	lemon juice	150 ml ($\frac{1}{4}$ pint)
50 g (2 oz)	blue cheese	75 g (3 oz)
5 ml (1 level tsp)	sugar	7·5 ml ($1\frac{1}{2}$ level tsp)
2·5 ml ($\frac{1}{2}$ level tsp)	salt	3·75 ml ($\frac{3}{4}$ level tsp)

Break the lettuce into chunks, wash and dry it. Place in a bowl with the radishes and spring onions and put the shrimps on top of the salad. Make up the dressing with the oil, lemon juice, blue cheese, sugar and salt. Blend these ingredients – if you do not have a blender, use a rotary whisk – until the sauce is smooth and creamy. Pour the dressing over and serve.

GUACAMOLE

Illustrated on the cover

They developed this spicy avocado pâté in Mexico, where the avocado was first grown. It must be one of the prettiest of starters, as well as pleasing most tastes.

Serves 4		Serves 6
2	ripe avocados	3
4	spring onions, trimmed	6
1	red *or* green pepper, seeded	1
4	tomatoes, skinned	6
15 ml (1 tbsp)	vegetable oil	30 ml (2 tbsp)
30 ml (2 tbsp)	lemon juice	45 ml (3 tbsp)
	salt and freshly ground pepper	
1·25 ml ($\frac{1}{4}$ level tsp)	chilli powder	1·25 ml ($\frac{1}{4}$ level tsp)

Peel, stone and mash the avocados in a glass or china bowl – using stainless steel tools (to avoid discolouration). Alternatively, scoop out the flesh if you wish to serve the Guacamole in the shells. Finely chop the onions, pepper and tomatoes. Add these with the oil, lemon juice, seasoning and chilli powder to the avocados. (A blender will do the job all at once, but don't let it get too smooth; it needs some crunch.) Pile the mixture into bowls or the avocado shells and chill. Garnish with pepper rings, if liked.

Thin crisp toast is nice with this – or celery sticks.

COLD CUCUMBER SOUP

A superb dish from the Middle East. Served cold this soup is cooling in the summer, warming served hot in the winter – it's also quick and easy to make.

Serves 4		Serves 6
1	cucumber	1 large
1 small	onion, skinned	1 medium
15 ml (1 tbsp)	vegetable oil	20 ml (4 tsp)
400 ml ($\frac{3}{4}$ pint)	chicken stock (a stock cube will do)	600 ml (1 pint)
300 ml ($\frac{1}{2}$ pint)	natural yogurt	400 ml ($\frac{3}{4}$ pint)
	salt and freshly ground pepper	
	fresh mint leaves to garnish	

Grate the unpeeled cucumber and the onion and fry both gently in the oil for 5 minutes. Add the chicken stock, bring to the boil, remove from the heat and stir in the yogurt carefully.

Season and serve garnished with mint leaves, or chill and serve cold for summer supper parties.

SPROUTS POLONAISE

The French have a habit of calling dishes with certain combinations of ingredients after other countries. Hard-boiled eggs and breadcrumbs are supposed to be Poland's style. But even if this dish never saw much of Warsaw, it still makes a stunningly good starter, and one that's perfect for slimmers too.

Serves 4		Serves 6
450 g (1 lb)	Brussels sprouts, trimmed	700 g ($1\frac{1}{2}$ lb)
75 g (3 oz)	fresh white breadcrumbs	100 g (4 oz)
50 g (2 oz)	butter	75 g (3 oz)
5 ml (1 level tsp)	garlic salt	7·5 ml ($1\frac{1}{2}$ level tsp)
2	hard-boiled eggs	3
	black pepper	

Cook the sprouts for 8 minutes in boiling salted water, then drain and keep warm. Fry the breadcrumbs in half the butter until brown. Add the garlic salt. Separate the yolks and the whites of the hard-boiled eggs and chop the whites up. Melt the rest of the butter in a frying pan, add the sprouts and sizzle for 1 minute. Add the breadcrumbs and egg white and put in a serving dish.

Cover with the crumbled egg yolks and serve with plenty of black pepper.

SMOKED HADDOCK MAYONNAISE

A creamy, lemony starter that's always a favourite, even with 'difficult' guests. Serve it straight from the dish with a lemon quarter each to squeeze over.

Serves 4		Serves 6
450 g (1 lb)	smoked haddock	700 g (1½ lb)
150 ml (¼ pint)	milk	225 ml (8 fl oz)
150 ml (¼ pint)	water	225 ml (8 fl oz)
15 ml (1 level tbsp)	flour	30 ml (2 level tbsp)
25 g (1 oz)	butter	40 g (1½ oz)
	salt and freshly ground pepper	
60 ml (4 tbsp)	mayonnaise	90 ml (6 tbsp)
15 ml (1 tbsp)	lemon juice	30 ml (2 tbsp)

Poach the haddock, covered, in the milk and water until tender – 8 minutes. Remove the fish from the pan, reserving liquid; skin and bone the fish and flake finely with a fork. Whisk the flour and butter into the cooking liquid and bring to the boil, when it should thicken. Add to the fish, season (easy on the salt), stir in the mayonnaise and lemon juice and put in a soufflé dish. Smooth the top and chill for at least 2 hours.

Granary bread is fabulous with this.

SALMON PÂTÉ

Incredibly rich, yet amazingly crafty – this is one of the grandest dishes I know. A special start for that special meal.

Serves 4		Serves 6
450 g (1 lb)	salmon (canned will do but it's not so nice)	700 g (1½ lb)
225 g (8 oz)	unsalted butter	350 g (12 oz)
30 ml (2 tbsp)	lemon juice	45 ml (3 tbsp)
	salt and freshly ground pepper	
60 ml (4 tbsp)	chopped fresh parsley	90 ml (6 tbsp)

Poach the salmon in just boiling water to cover, for 5 minutes.

Leave to cool in the liquid for 2 hours; skin, bone and flake the fish. Melt the butter and stir all but about one eighth into the salmon. Add the lemon juice, season and add the parsley. Stir until mixed, put in a soufflé dish and seal with the remaining butter. A blender gives this too smooth a texture for my taste, but could be used.

This just begs for lots of hot brown toast – don't deny it its due!

PUMPKIN AND LEEK SOUP

A winter soup this – golden and glowing in colour, warming and creamy to the taste. It comes from the southern states of America but has its origins in Europe, away to the south again.

Serves 4		Serves 6
450 g (1 lb)	pumpkin, seeded	700 g (1½ lb)
225 g (8 oz)	leeks, trimmed	350 g (12 oz)
50 g (2 oz)	butter	75 g (3 oz)
1·1 litres (2 pints)	chicken stock	1·7 litres (3 pints)
	salt and freshly ground pepper	
60 ml (4 tbsp)	single or double cream	90 ml (6 tbsp)

Don't peel the pumpkin but wash and cut into 1-cm ($\frac{1}{2}$-in) cubes. Wash the leeks thoroughly, then slice thinly and add with the pumpkin to the butter. Fry for 3 minutes, add the stock and simmer for 25 minutes. Liquidise or sieve. Season and stir in the cream.

Home-made croûtons are a great favourite with this.

SHRIMPS WITH MELON

Frozen melon balls are one of the great standbys. You can have a small packet of frozen shrimps waiting next to them in the freezer for the unexpected guest or for those times when you really don't have the extra energy to struggle with all three courses. This is a real goodie.

Serves 4		Serves 6
225 g (8 oz)	melon balls, fresh or frozen	275 g (10 oz)
175 g (6 oz)	shrimps, peeled	225 g (8 oz)
1	lettuce, shredded	1
150 ml ($\frac{1}{4}$ pint)	mayonnaise (Hellmann's is best for this)	225 ml (8 fl oz)
	For the dressing	
60 ml (4 tbsp)	vegetable oil	90 ml (6 tbsp)
30 ml (2 tbsp)	lemon juice	45 ml (3 tbsp)
5 ml (1 level tsp)	salt	7·5 ml (1$\frac{1}{2}$ level tsp)
5 ml (1 level tsp)	sugar	7·5 ml (1$\frac{1}{2}$ level tsp)

Whisk the vegetable oil, lemon juice, salt and sugar together to make the lemon dressing. Mix the melon balls and shrimps with the dressing, saving a few shrimps for decoration. Chill it and serve in lettuce-lined wine glasses. Spoon over mayonnaise and decorate with spare shrimps.

Thinly cut brown bread and butter is the perfect foil.

TAGLIATELLE WITH TUNA SAUCE

This incorporates the crafty way of cooking pasta, with a dead simple sauce that looks as pretty as it tastes. Green noodles are fine for this – yellow ones are okay.

Serves 4		Serves 6
225 g (8 oz)	tagliatelle (flat egg noodles)	350 g (12 oz)
2·3 litres (4 pints)	water	2·8 litres (5 pints)
198-g (7-oz)	can tuna, drained	198-g (7-oz)
298-g (10$\frac{1}{2}$-oz)	can condensed mushroom soup	298-g (10$\frac{1}{2}$-oz)
100-g (4-oz)	packet frozen mixed vegetables	226-g (8-oz)
1·25 ml ($\frac{1}{4}$ level tsp)	salt	2·5 ml ($\frac{1}{2}$ level tsp)
	freshly ground pepper	
60 ml (4 tbsp)	chicken stock	90 ml (6 tbsp)
25 g (1 oz)	butter	50 g (2 oz)
10 ml (2 tsp)	lemon juice	15 ml (1 tbsp)
30 ml (2 tbsp)	grated Parmesan cheese	60 ml (4 tbsp)

Put the noodles into boiling salted water and boil for 3 minutes. Put on the lid, take off heat and leave for 7 minutes – when they will be perfect. Meanwhile, flake the tuna. Heat the soup – *undiluted* – with the vegetables, seasoning and stock, and add the butter, tuna and lemon juice.

Drain the noodles, pour over the sauce and sprinkle with Parmesan – Cheddar will do, but it's not the same.

GAZPACHO

In Southern Spain where it comes from, there are no hard and fast rules for this famous cold soup – experiment yourself – let your guests choose from a variety of accompaniments.

Serves 4		Serves 6
600 ml (1 pint)	tomato juice	900 ml (1½ pints)
300 ml (½ pint)	water	600 ml (1 pint)
30 ml (2 tbsp)	vegetable oil	45 ml (3 tbsp)
30 ml (2 tbsp)	wine *or* cider vinegar	45 ml (3 tbsp)
1	tomato, skinned and chopped	2
5 ml (1 level tsp)	garlic salt	7·5 ml (1½ level tsp)
	ice cubes	

To serve, a selection of chopped tomato; onion; green pepper; grated cucumber; celery; bread cubes; black or green olives, stoned

Mix tomato juice, water, oil and vinegar together. Add the chopped tomato, the garlic salt and cubes of ice (2 to a person).

Serve with chopped and grated vegetables and bread cut into cubes, arranged in bowls so your guests can help themselves and make their own taste sensations by mixing with the basic soup.

PROVENÇALE FISH SOUP

All the scents and savours of a Mediterranean meal are epitomised for me in this soup, with its subtle sea flavours and hint of garlic. For the fish, heads and trimmings really are all you need.

Serves 4		Serves 6
1·1 kg (2½ lb)	fish heads and trimmings	1·6 kg (3½ lb)
1·1 litres (2 pints)	water	1·7 litres (3 pints)
1	bay leaf	2
226-g (8-oz)	can tomatoes	396-g (14-oz)
1	clove of garlic, skinned and crushed	2
15 ml (1 tbsp)	vegetable oil	30 ml (2 tbsp)
	salt and freshly ground pepper	

Simmer the fish trimmings in the water with the bay leaf for 30 minutes. Strain and return any fish to the stock with the canned tomatoes, garlic and oil. Blend for 30 seconds (or rub through a sieve), season and bring to the boil. Simmer for 5 minutes.

Serve with oven toasted bread.

BEEF LINDSTROM

An unusual Swedish recipe that everyone seems to like. Perfect for stretching a little spare minced beef to feed four.

Serves 4		Serves 6
225 g (8 oz)	cooked beetroot, skinned	350 g (12 oz)
60 ml (4 tbsp)	natural yogurt	90 ml (6 tbsp)
15 ml (1 level tbsp)	mild mustard	25 ml (1½ level tbsp)
100 g (4 oz)	minced beef	175 g (6 oz)
	salt and freshly ground pepper	
4 thin slices	buttered brown toast	6 thin slices
	watercress to garnish	

Grate the beetroot and mix with the yogurt, mustard and beef. Season and spread on buttered toast slices. Put under a hot grill for 5 minutes. Serve garnished with watercress. It's nice cut into fingers to have with drinks, too.

CRAB TART

This is a grand starter both in appearance and taste. It is not cheap, but can make up for a lot of shortcuts when you're rushed, or set off a really great party.

Serves 4		Serves 6
175 g (6 oz)	shortcrust pastry (home-made or packet)	225 g (8 oz)
2	eggs	2
1	egg yolk	2
225 g (8 oz)	crab meat	225 g (8 oz)
150 ml (¼ pint)	single cream	300 ml (½ pint)
	salt and freshly ground pepper	

Roll out the pastry and use to line a 20·5-cm (8-in) or 25·5-cm (10-in) flan dish (preferably with a removable base). Prick the pastry and put some foil in the centre with rice or beans to weight it down. Bake for 15 minutes at 200°C (400°F) mark 6. Beat the whole eggs and egg yolk with the crab meat, cream and seasonings and pour into the pastry case (having first removed the foil). Bake at 190°C (375°F) mark 5 for 25 minutes.

It's marvellous served hot, but still pretty good to eat cold.

KIPPERS MICHELIN

I first had these kippers at the launch of one of the renowned Michelin Guides. It just shows what an unorthodox approach can do with a food we thought we knew all about. Don't be tempted to cook the kippers!

Serves 4		Serves 6
4	kipper fillets	6
1 medium	Spanish onion, skinned	1 large
90 ml (6 tbsp)	oil (preferably olive)	135 ml (9 tbsp)
45 ml (3 tbsp)	lemon juice	75 ml (5 tbsp)
1 small	lettuce	1 large
	freshly ground black pepper	

Slice the kipper fillets diagonally into 0·5-cm (¼-in) slices. Slice the onion into very thin rings. Mix with the kippers and cover with oil and lemon juice. Marinate for at least 2 hours and serve on a bed of shredded lettuce with plenty of freshly ground black pepper.

Brown bread is best with this.

DANISH SOUSED HERRINGS

A touch of sweet and sour makes these herrings an unusual first course. Or do as the Danes do, serve them with lots of other delicacies as part of a smörgasbord.

Serves 4		Serves 6
300 ml (½ pint)	cider *or* wine vinegar	400 ml (¾ pint)
30 ml (2 level tbsp)	sugar	45 ml (3 level tbsp)
15 ml (1 level tbsp)	salt	20 ml (4 level tsp)
15 ml (1 level tbsp)	pickling spice	20 ml (4 level tsp)
450 g (1 lb)	herring fillets	700 g (1½ lb)

Bring the vinegar to the boil and add the sugar and seasonings. Simmer for 5 minutes. Add the herrings and boil for 1 minute. Put the mixture in a flat dish and chill for 24 hours. Up to 3 days is okay – so too is a sliced onion in the vinegar.

To serve, remove the fillets and pour over a little of the strained vinegar. Decorate the dish with some green herbs if you have them and serve with rye or pumpernickel bread.

SMOKED MACKEREL PÂTÉ

This is probably my favourite fish starter. Always impressive and very easy to do, it's a shame to confine it to parties – I usually keep some in the fridge!

Serves 4		Serves 6
450 g (1 lb)	smoked mackerel fillets	700 g (1½ lb)
225 g (8 oz)	unsalted butter	350 g (12 oz)
60 ml (4 tbsp)	lemon juice	90 ml (6 tbsp)
2·5 ml (½ level tsp)	ground nutmeg	3·75 ml (¾ level tsp)
	salt and freshly ground pepper	

Skin and mash the mackerel, removing any visible bones. Melt the butter and stir into the mackerel, keeping back 30 ml (2 tbsp). Beat until smooth – very easy with the hot butter. Add the juice and nutmeg. Season carefully (watch the salt), and pack into pretty dishes. Seal with the remaining butter. Chill for at least 2 hours.

Just fabulous with wholemeal toast – not bad as a sandwich filler either.

SMOKED SALMON SCRAMBLE

A tasty way of making a little expensive smoked salmon go further and still taste terrific. Some shops and market stalls sell 'off-cuts', which are fine for this when you take the skin off.

Serves 4		Serves 6
50 g (2 oz)	butter	75 g (3 oz)
50 g (2 oz)	smoked salmon	75 g (3 oz)
8	eggs	12
	salt and freshly ground pepper	
60 ml (4 tbsp)	soured cream	150 ml ($\frac{1}{4}$ pint)

Melt the butter and add the salmon cut into small pieces – stir for 1 minute. Beat the eggs with the seasoning, add them to the salmon and scramble gently until cooked but (ideally) still soft.

Serve on wholemeal toast with 15 ml (1 tbsp) soured cream on each serving.

EGGS IN ASPIC

This needs to be done in advance, but will keep for a day in the fridge. Don't over-cook the eggs – the still creamy yolk is one of the great pleasures and surprises.

Serves 4		Serves 6
4	eggs	6
298-g (10$\frac{1}{2}$-oz)	can condensed consommé	two 298-g (10$\frac{1}{2}$-oz)
8	parsley sprigs	12

Put the eggs in boiling water for exactly 5 minutes; take out and cool in cold water. Craze the shell with a spoon and shell very carefully – the yolks are still creamy. Melt the consommé and put 15 ml (1 tbsp) in the base of 4 (6) baby soufflé dishes. Chill until set. Add the parsley sprigs to each dish, then the eggs and pour over the consommé to cover the eggs. Set in the fridge for at least 2 hours. To unmould, loosen top with a knife round the edge, dip the bottom of the dishes in hot water for just 15 seconds and then turn out on to plates.

Some finely sliced cucumber is nice with this.

CURRIED APPLE SOUP

This is one of my favourite summer soups. Very easy to make, with a combination of unusual flavours that makes it a talking point at any meal.

Serves 4		Serves 6
450 g (1 lb)	cooking apples	700 g (1$\frac{1}{2}$ lb)
50 g (2 oz)	butter	75 g (3 oz)
1 large	onion, skinned and chopped	2 medium
15 ml (1 level tbsp)	mild curry powder	20 ml (4 level tsp)
900 ml (1$\frac{1}{2}$ pints)	chicken stock	1·3 litres (2$\frac{1}{4}$ pints)
pinch	ground cinnamon	pinch
	salt and freshly ground pepper	

Core, but don't peel the apples. Cut them into small pieces. Melt the butter in a pan and add the apple and onion. Turn until coated, then add the curry powder. Cook very gently for 2–3 minutes. Add the chicken stock, bring to the boil and simmer for 15 minutes. Liquidise the mixture and season with a generous pinch of cinnamon and salt and pepper. Leave to cool and then place in the fridge until thoroughly chilled. It can be served as it is or with a generous dollop of natural yogurt in each bowl, or with tiny cubes of eating apple – red or green skin left on, floating on the surface.

STUFFED THREE DELICIOUS

A Chinese-style name for one of the simplest and most delicious of all egg recipes. If you haven't got the exact ingredients you can always improvise, but keep the colours separate.

Serves 4		Serves 6
6	hard-boiled eggs	9
60-g (2-oz)	can anchovies, drained and mashed	60-g (2-oz)
15 ml (1 level tbsp)	tomato paste	20 ml (4 level tsp)
30 ml (2 level tbsp)	mango chutney	45 ml (3 level tbsp)
15 ml (1 level tbsp)	grainy French mustard	20 ml (4 level tsp)
15 ml (1 tbsp)	mayonnaise	20 ml (4 tsp)
	chopped parsley	

Halve the eggs lengthways and remove the yolks into 3 bowls – a third in each bowl. To one bowl add the anchovies and tomato paste; the chutney to the next; and the mustard and mayonnaise to the third. Blend each until smooth and refill the whites, mounding up the filling.

Serve sprinkled with parsley and with French bread, one of each flavour per person.

QUICK GREEN PEA SOUP

This is really a freezer standby, as all the ingredients can be kept for months in your freezer, ready to go and there's no need to thaw them first.

Serves 4		Serves 6
1·4 litres (2½ pints)	chicken stock	2 litres (3½ pints)
450 g (1 lb)	frozen peas (not minted)	700 g (1½ lb)
1 small	onion, skinned and chopped (optional)	1 large
50 g (2 oz)	butter	75 g (3 oz)
	salt and freshly ground pepper	
15 ml (1 level tbsp)	cornflour	20 ml (4 level tsp)
30 ml (2 tbsp)	vegetable oil	45 ml (3 tbsp)
2 slices	bread, cut into 1-cm (½-in) cubes	3 slices

Put the chicken stock in a saucepan and bring it to a rolling boil. Add the peas and cook through for 4–5 minutes. If you like the flavour, you can add the onion at this stage. Add the butter, and when it's melted put the mixture into a liquidiser and blend until smooth. Return to the saucepan and season well. Blend the cornflour with a little water, add to the soup and reheat until thickened.

In a small frying pan, heat the oil and carefully fry the 1-cm (½-in) bread cubes until they are a light golden brown. Serve the soup and the bread croûtons separately, dropping the croûtons into the soup at the last minute when they will hiss and crackle and provide a lovely crunchy contrast to the creamy smooth texture of the soup. You can also add a few tablespoonfuls of cream or top of the milk to the soup just before serving. I think it's an improvement as it helps to break down the improbable green colour that the frozen peas give it. It also helps the flavour, though that's pretty good to start with.

EGGS AND ARTICHOKES

A good standby starter, this: with eggs in the fridge and a tin of artichokes in your larder, it can be turned out almost instantaneously. Don't disregard it because of that though. The flavours and textures complement each other in a quite unusual way. A few strips of anchovy fillet across the eggs add an unusual sharpness and piquancy to the dish if you fancy the thought.

Serves 4		Serves 6
4	hard-boiled eggs	6
396-g (14-oz)	can artichoke hearts	396-g (14-oz)
15 ml (1 tbsp)	lemon juice	30 ml (2 tbsp)
300 ml ($\frac{1}{2}$ pint)	mayonnaise (see page 40)	400 ml ($\frac{3}{4}$ pint)

Shell and halve the eggs. (Use a stainless knife with its blade dipped in cold water.) Drain and rinse the artichokes thoroughly. Arrange them with the eggs on an oval dish. Mix the lemon juice with the mayonnaise and pour over. Chill for 15 minutes.

FRENCH COUNTRY VEGETABLE SOUP

This is the classic soup of France. Some of my earliest memories of French food are connected with a great tureen of this soup, which used to appear at dinner every evening in a hotel where we were staying, in a France still recovering from the ravages of war. Its rich flavour and earthy comfort have always been symbolic to me ever since. The best in French cooking.

Serves 4		Serves 6
225 g (8 oz)	potatoes, peeled	350 g (12 oz)
225 g (8 oz)	carrots, peeled	350 g (12 oz)
1 large	onion, skinned	2 medium
225 g (8 oz)	leeks, trimmed	350 g (12 oz)
50 g (2 oz)	butter	75 g (3 oz)
5 ml (1 level tsp)	salt	7·5 ml (1$\frac{1}{2}$ level tsp)
	freshly ground pepper	
1·1 litres (2 pints)	chicken stock	1·7 litres (3 pints)

Grate, on a coarse blade of the grater, the potatoes and carrots and the onion. Wash the leeks carefully and chop them finely, saving a few shreds of the green part for garnish later. Fry all the vegetables gently in the butter in a large saucepan for about 8–9 minutes, not letting them brown, but just cooking lightly until they and the butter absorb each other's flavours. Add the salt and a good sprinkling of pepper. Pour on the chicken stock, bring to the boil and simmer for 20 minutes. The soup, after seasoning, is now ready to serve.

Into each bowl put a knob of butter and a little finely chopped parsley to get the perfect authentic French effect. You can, if you like your soups really smooth, put the mixture into the liquidiser, but I personally prefer the slightly grainy and more authentic texture you get from the grating and fine chopping. The few shreds of green leek can be sprinkled over the top as the soup is being served.

Crusty French bread turns this into a meal of real rustic charm.

Forty Delicious Desserts

PEARS BELLE HÉLÈNE

The only reason I can think of why this is called after Helen of Troy is not exactly polite. But as we all know, the ideal female figure has changed a lot down the centuries. I suggest you make up your own explanation but don't forget to serve this dish on a special occasion. It could launch quite a few ships itself.

Serves 4		Serves 6
2	ripe pears, peeled	3
300 ml ($\frac{1}{2}$ pint)	water	400 ml ($\frac{3}{4}$ pint)
150 g (5 oz)	sugar	200 g (7 oz)
450 ml (17 fl oz)	vanilla ice cream	700 ml ($1\frac{1}{4}$ pints)
283-g (10-oz)	bottle chocolate sauce	283-g (10-oz)

Halve the pears and remove the cores. Simmer in a syrup made from the water and sugar for 5 minutes. Cool. (If you are pushed, you can use tinned pears – but they are not as nice.)

Put half a pear on each portion of ice cream. Heat the chocolate sauce and, just before serving, pour the sauce over.

Serve very quickly!

PEACH MELBA

This dish was invented, so legend has it, for the great Australian opera singer, Nellie Melba, as it both catered for her sweet tooth and soothed her over-used tonsils. What you do with your tonsils is your own business; I think the flavours in this classic pudding are worth a song or two themselves.

Serves 4		Serves 6
2	fresh peaches (*or* peach halves, canned or frozen)	3
45 ml (3 level tbsp)	sugar	60 ml (4 level tbsp)
150 ml ($\frac{1}{4}$ pint)	water	175 ml (6 fl oz)
450 ml (17 fl oz)	vanilla ice cream	700 ml ($1\frac{1}{4}$ pints)
	For the raspberry syrup	
100 g (4 oz)	raspberries	175 g (6 oz)
60 ml (4 level tbsp)	sugar	90 ml (6 level tbsp)

If you are using fresh peaches – and they are far the nicest – dip them for just 30 seconds in boiling water, after which the skins will slide off. Cut them in half, take out the stones and poach the halves in a syrup made with the sugar and water boiled together for no more than 8 minutes. Let them cool. For the raspberry syrup, simmer the raspberries and sugar together, without any water, for 10 minutes. When you are ready to serve, put a mound of the ice cream in the bottom of each glass dish, a peach half on top of it (cut-side down) and pour over some raspberry syrup.

Although it's not traditional, I like serving this syrup hot over the cold peach and ice cream. It looks almost as good as it tastes.

GRANITA LEMONE

This recipe's so easy I always think it's cheating. But the guests never do. The secret is to assure them it was nothing – they will never believe you, even though it's almost true. Don't forget the grated peel, it makes all the difference to your credibility.

Serves 4		Serves 6
4	lemons	6
300–400 ml (10–15 fl oz)	lemon water ice – bought from a freezer centre	400–600 ml (15–20 fl oz)

Cut one end off each lemon like a lid. Scoop out the pulp, trim the bottoms so they stand upright, and fill with water ice. Grate the peel from 2 of the lids over the lemons and cut a pretty sliver from the 2 remaining lids to stick in the top of each one.

Put the lemons in your freezer compartment and take out 10 minutes before serving. Don't let on!

They can be served in big egg cups if you've got pretty ones.

COMPOTE OF ORANGES

This is one of the simplest of puddings, yet is always a great favourite. Presentation is all important. Tall wine glasses bring out the delicate golden colour of the oranges in their syrup, and the lovely marbling effect you get when you pour in the cream.

Serves 4		Serves 6
250 g (9 oz)	caster sugar	350 g (12 oz)
300 ml (½ pint)	water	400 ml (¾ pint)
4	oranges, thinly sliced – not peeled	6

Boil the sugar and water until it is clear – about 5 minutes should do it. Cool slightly and add the orange slices. Simmer until the peel goes a little transparent – about 10 minutes – *don't boil hard.*

Leave to cool in the syrup.

Serve oranges and syrup with single cream in tall glasses.

ROYAL CREAM

Legend has it this was one of Queen Victoria's favourites. Maybe it even raised a smile. It'll certainly do that for your guests. Not a dish to serve after too rich a main course and starter though, unless you want to carry your guests from table to armchair.

Serves 4		Serves 6
50 g (2 oz)	macaroons *or* ground almonds	75 g (3 oz)
15 ml (1 level tbsp)	cornflour	30 ml (2 level tbsp)
75 g (3 oz)	sugar	115 g (4½ oz)
4	egg yolks	6
568 ml (1 pint)	milk	900 ml (1½ pints)
150 ml (¼ pint)	double cream	225 ml (8 fl oz)
	toasted almonds to decorate	

Crush the macaroons to a fine powder (or use ground almonds) and mix with the cornflour, sugar and egg yolks. Boil the milk and pour, still hot, over the almond mixture. Stir this gently over the heat until it is smooth and thick. *Do not boil it.* Add the gently whipped cream and put the whole mixture in a pretty dish.

Chill and serve decorated with toasted almonds.

CRÈME CARAMEL

In France they also call this dish Crème renversée, which means that it's got to be turned out. The extraordinary thing is that the caramel turns into a sauce while the custard cooks. It's worth trying this one on your own first, just to make sure you don't wind up with pouring custard or scrambled eggs.

Serves 4		Serves 6
	For the caramel	
75 g (3 oz)	sugar	100 g (4 oz)
75 ml (3 fl oz)	water	100 ml (4 fl oz)
	For the custard	
300 ml ($\frac{1}{2}$ pint)	milk	400 ml ($\frac{3}{4}$ pint)
300 ml ($\frac{1}{2}$ pint)	evaporated milk	400 ml ($\frac{3}{4}$ pint)
2	eggs	3
2	egg yolks	3
45 ml (3 level tbsp)	sugar	60 ml (4 level tbsp)
5 ml (1 tsp)	vanilla essence	7·5 ml ($1\frac{1}{2}$ tsp)

For the caramel, mix the sugar and water together in a pan until the sugar melts. Then bring to the boil and cook until it starts to caramelise (when it smells like toffee and turns dark brown). But do not burn. Pour, still hot, into the bottom of 4 (6) baby soufflé dishes. Bring the milk and evaporated milk to the boil in a saucepan then take off the heat. Beat the whole eggs and egg yolks together with the sugar and vanilla essence. Add the milk, beating steadily until the mixture is smooth. Strain the custard through a sieve into the soufflé dishes. Put them in a baking tray with hot water half way up their sides and cook at 160°C (325°F) mark 3 for about 35–45 minutes, until set. Allow to cool, chill in the refrigerator, and turn out before serving.

They should be set, but smooth and creamy inside, with the caramel forming a sauce over and around them.

COFFEE CREAM CHEESE

Deceptively simple this one. It takes no more than a minute to do and is perfect for a rather special pudding made in a rush.

Serves 4		Serves 6
50 g (2 oz)	caster sugar	75 g (3 oz)
25 ml (1½ level tbsp)	instant coffee	30 ml (2 level tbsp)
225 ml (8 fl oz)	boiling water	350 ml (12 fl oz)
225 g (8 oz)	'Philadelphia' *or* other cream cheese	350 g (12 oz)

Dissolve the sugar and coffee in the water and, while still warm, beat carefully into the cheese. Pile it into wine glasses.

Chill and serve with wafer thin biscuits and a little single cream over the top if you are feeling extravagant.

GINGER ICE CREAM

This is one of those delicious American sauces for ice cream. It's incredibly easy to do and yet always brings compliments for the combination of sweet and spicy, hot and cold, smooth and crunchy.

Serves 4		Serves 6
50 g (2 oz)	preserved ginger and syrup	75 g (3 oz)
15 ml (1 tbsp)	honey	30 ml (2 tbsp)
450 ml (17 fl oz)	vanilla ice cream (preferably Cornish-type)	700 ml (1¼ pints)

Chop the ginger pieces finely and heat them in their syrup with the honey. Pour over dishes of ice cream and serve quickly.

Gingernuts are fun with this. A single large piece of ginger embedded in the ice cream is nice too.

CINNAMON PEARS

This is one of those dishes you can make with what you've got in the larder, and still have people going 'Ooh, ahh!'. But it's worth buying the food specially too, because it just tastes so good.

Serves 4		Serves 6
4	pears, peeled, halved and cored (*or* canned)	
60 ml (4 level tbsp)	desiccated coconut	90 ml (6 level tbsp)
5 ml (1 level tsp)	ground cinnamon	7·5 ml (1½ level tsp)
5 ml (1 level tsp)	cornflour	7·5 ml (1½ level tsp)
150 ml (¼ pint)	pear juice *or*	200 ml (7 fl oz)
150 ml (¼ pint)	water, and	200 ml (7 fl oz)
30 ml (2 level tbsp)	sugar	45 ml (3 level tbsp)
7 g (¼ oz)	butter	15 g (½ oz)

Place the 8 (12) pear halves face downwards in a buttered baking dish. Sprinkle 15 ml (1 level tbsp) desiccated coconut over each pear and bake for 10 minutes at 180°C (350°F) mark 4. Mix the cinnamon and cornflour with the pear syrup (or syrup made with the water and sugar). Bring to the boil, stir until thick, add a small knob of butter, then pour over the pears and serve.

Disgustingly fattening but very delicious.

CARAMEL ORANGES

Oranges like this are one of the main attractions of every good restaurant's dessert trolley. Even if you're not preparing a trolley full of sweets, the gentle toffee flavour, the candied peel and the still fresh oranges are really quite sensational.

Serves 4		Serves 6
4	oranges, seedless if possible	6
225 g (8 oz)	sugar	350 g (12 oz)
300 ml ($\frac{1}{2}$ pint)	water	400 ml ($\frac{3}{4}$ pint)

Peel the oranges carefully, removing the white pith. Mix the sugar and water and boil. Turn the peeled oranges in this mixture for 3–4 minutes, then remove. Cut the peel of one orange into matchstick-size slivers, add to the syrup and boil until it *begins* to turn brown. Pour the syrup and peel slivers over the oranges and chill.

Serve them with single cream and a knife and fork.

BLACKBERRY COBBLER

This is an autumn pudding. Even if you make it in the spring with frozen blackberries it's still an autumn pudding. The smell and richness always remind me of the golden days at the beginning of leaf fall.

Serves 4		Serves 6
450 g (1 lb)	blackberries (frozen will do)	700 g ($1\frac{1}{2}$ lb)
225 g (8 oz)	sugar	350 g (12 oz)
100 g (4 oz)	self raising flour	175 g (6 oz)
1	egg, beaten	1
15 ml (1 tbsp)	oil	20 ml (4 tsp)
200 ml (7 fl oz)	milk	300 ml ($\frac{1}{2}$ pint)

Mix the blackberries with half the sugar and put into an oval casserole. Mix the flour, egg, remaining sugar, oil and enough of the milk to make a very thick batter – only just runny. Pour over the blackberries. Bake for 35 minutes at 190°C (375°F) mark 5.

Serve with home-made custard or thick cream.

ORANGE FOOL

Illustrated on the cover

This is an adaptation of a recipe originally developed in one of the great gentlemen's clubs of St James's, 'Boodles', but much too good to be allowed to remain there. 'Fool' is a curious word applied to a number of dishes based on fruit purées, dating back to the seventeenth century, but there's nothing silly about this splendidly easy dessert.

Serves 4		Serves 6
300 ml ($\frac{1}{2}$ pint)	double cream	400 ml ($\frac{3}{4}$ pint)
300 ml ($\frac{1}{2}$ pint)	orange juice	400 ml ($\frac{3}{4}$ pint)
225 g (8 oz)	sponge cake (dry is fine)	350 g (12 oz)
	grated rind of 1 orange	

Whip the cream lightly and mix with half the orange juice. Soak the cake in the remaining orange juice and pour the cream over it. Sprinkle with the orange rind and chill. You may want to sweeten the cream if the juice is not very sweet.

It looks pretty served in individual portions in big wine glasses.

BAKED CODLINGS

A 'codling' is an apple, just in case you were wondering what this recipe is doing in the puddings. Don't be tempted to use cooking apples for it. The texture and scent you get with ripe eating apples is an absolute revelation.

Serves 4		Serves 6
4	large Cox's-type apples	6
100 g (4 oz)	butter	175 g (6 oz)
50 g (2 oz)	brown sugar	75 g (3 oz)
50 g (2 oz)	sultanas	75 g (3 oz)
	ground nutmeg	

Core, but don't peel the apples. Stuff them with the butter, sugar, sultanas and nutmeg. Put them into a baking tin with 1 cm ($\frac{1}{2}$ in) of water in it.

Bake for 35–40 minutes, at 180°C (350°F) mark 4.
Serve with the juice from the pan poured over them and whipped cream.

ICE CREAM WITH STRAWBERRY SAUCE

I never really get tired of eating strawberries just with sugar and cream; but when they're too expensive or just too common to eat like that, try this recipe with strawberries on top of cream instead of vice versa.

Serves 4		Serves 6
225 g (8 oz)	strawberries, hulled	350 g (12 oz)
25 g (1 oz)	butter	50 g (2 oz)
15 ml (1 level tbsp)	sugar	20 ml (4 level tsp)
30 ml (2 tbsp)	lemon juice	45 ml (3 tbsp)
450 ml (17 fl oz)	Cornish vanilla ice cream	700 ml ($1\frac{1}{4}$ pints)

Slice the strawberries into 0·5-cm ($\frac{1}{4}$-in) slices. Heat the butter, sugar and lemon juice together in a pan until the mixture is bubbling, but *not* brown. Add the strawberries and simmer for 2 minutes only, until the sauce has turned straw-berry coloured. Put the ice cream into wine glasses. Pour the sauce over the ice cream and eat it very quickly.

Almond biscuits are nice with this.

APPLE PANCAKES

These small and incredibly scrumptious pancakes originally come from Normandy where they're known as Jacques. They're a really fabulous ending to a friendly supper party, but I sometimes make them on their own as a snack for hungry – or just greedy – friends.

Serves 4		Serves 6
1 large	cooking apple	2 medium
100 g (4 oz)	plain flour	175 g (6 oz)
50 g (2 oz)	caster sugar	75 g (3 oz)
1	egg, beaten	1
15 ml (1 tbsp)	vegetable oil	30 ml (2 tbsp)
pinch	salt	pinch
200 ml (7 fl oz)	orange juice	300 ml ($\frac{1}{2}$ pint)

Core, *don't* peel, and grate the apple. Mix the flour, sugar, egg, 5 ml (1 tsp) oil and salt together. Beat in the orange juice to make a thick cream. Add the apple and fry 15 ml (1 tbsp) at a time in a thick frying pan brushed with oil. Turn over when brown – after about 2–3 minutes.

Serve sandwiched with butter, apple jelly or honey – and with thick cream.

Don't eat too many!

ANANAS SAUVAGE

This recipe may seem simple but the surprise effect of treating a pineapple like something totally different just highlights the texture and flavour that these very special fruits can have.

Serves 4		Serves 6
1 medium	ripe pineapple	1 large
60 ml (4 level tbsp)	sugar	90 ml (6 level tbsp)
30 ml (2 tbsp)	lemon juice	45 ml (3 tbsp)

Stand the pineapple on its bottom and cut into 4 (6) lengthways, slicing through the green top at the same time. Then cut the pineapple wedges as you would slice a melon: first slice carefully along under the skin, then cut each section into 1-cm ($\frac{1}{2}$-in) segments. Sprinkle with sugar and lemon juice and chill.

Serve with forks as well as spoons.

The 'sauvage' doesn't mean savage, in French it means wild!

65

MANGO FOOL

To the best of my knowledge, the Indians never developed this perfect finish to a hot, spicy meal. The combination of tangy mango purée and rich cream is just incomparable. It must be one of the ultimate desserts.

Serves 4		Serves 6
300 ml ($\frac{1}{2}$ pint)	double cream	400 ml ($\frac{3}{4}$ pint)
15 ml (1 level tbsp)	preserved ginger, chopped	30 ml (2 level tbsp)
15 ml (1 tbsp)	preserved ginger syrup	30 ml (2 tbsp)
454-g (16-oz)	can mango purée (preferably Indian)	700 g ($1\frac{1}{2}$ lb)
	or	
454-g (16-oz)	can mangoes, puréed	700 g ($1\frac{1}{2}$ lb)

Whip the cream until thick, but not grainy. Stir in the chopped ginger pieces and ginger syrup, and then the mango purée. Mix well together, folding carefully so as not to lose the bulk of the cream. Pour into tall elegant wine glasses and chill for at least $1\frac{1}{2}$ hours before serving.

If you can find the French almond biscuits called Tuiles to go with it, you should have a smile on your face for weeks afterwards.

ST CLEMENT'S SYLLABUB

An instant pudding with a refreshing flavour, despite its creaminess. Named after the old song 'Oranges and Lemons', it takes only five minutes to make and another thirty to set.

Serves 4		Serves 6
	grated rind and juice of 1 lemon	
	grated rind and juice of 1 orange	
2	juice of oranges	3
50–75 g (2–3 oz)	caster sugar	75–100 g (3–4 oz)
300 ml ($\frac{1}{2}$ pint)	double cream	400 ml ($\frac{3}{4}$ pint)

Mix the juices together with the sugar and whisk into the cream a quarter at a time, beating until thick but not stiff. Add the lemon rind.

Pour into wine glasses and decorate with orange rind – chill for at least 30 minutes.

FRENCH APPLE PUDDING

This is a pudding unlike any other I know – a kind of super thick apple pancake that cooks so easily it always amazes me how little trouble it takes.

Serves 4		Serves 6
450 g (1 lb)	cooking apples, peeled and cored	700 g ($1\frac{1}{2}$ lb)
50 g (2 oz)	butter	75 g (3 oz)
5 ml (1 level tsp)	ground cinnamon	7·5 ml ($1\frac{1}{2}$ level tsp)
50 g (2 oz)	caster sugar	75 g (3 oz)
200 ml (7 fl oz)	milk	250 ml (9 fl oz)
2	eggs, beaten	3
10 ml (2 tsp)	vanilla essence	10 ml (2 tsp)
60 ml (4 level tbsp)	icing sugar	90 ml (6 level tbsp)
75 g (3 oz)	flour	100 g (4 oz)
pinch	salt	pinch

Slice the apples and cook in the butter for 3 minutes. Add the cinnamon and sugar. Blend the milk, eggs and vanilla essence until smooth and add the icing sugar – a little at a time – whisking as you go. Then add the flour and salt in the same way. Pour into a greased baking tray or china flan dish, add the apples and bake for $1\frac{1}{4}$ hours at 180°C (350°F) mark 4.

Sprinkle sugar over and eat with lots of cream.

QUEEN'S PUDDING

This most unusual pudding, a variation of the baked Queen of Puddings, is made in a frying pan and good hot or cold. It is very rich but not cloying. A good end to a meal of sharp flavours and strong tastes.

Serves 4		Serves 6
300 ml ($\frac{1}{2}$ pint)	single cream	the same quantities
2	eggs	as for 4 servings.
2	egg yolks	
50 g (2 oz)	caster sugar	
2·5 ml ($\frac{1}{2}$ tsp)	almond essence	
50 g (2 oz)	ground almonds	
50 g (2 oz)	fresh white breadcrumbs	
25 g (1 oz)	butter	
	slivered almonds and glacé cherries to decorate	

Bring the cream to a boil and set aside. Beat the eggs, yolks, sugar and essence together until doubled in bulk. Add the cream steadily and whisk until smooth. Fold in the almonds and breadcrumbs with a metal spoon. Melt the butter in a deep frying pan and cook the mixture until it thickens and sets – 4–5 minutes.

Invert the pan and turn on to a serving plate; decorate with almonds and glacé cherries.

PANCAKES

Pancakes are all too often confined to Shrove Tuesday in this country, when we should be eating them all the year round. Here is a basic recipe and some fillings. Don't worry if the first pancake goes funny – it often does for experienced cooks too.

Serves 4		Serves 6
1	egg	1
15 ml (1 tbsp)	vegetable oil	30 ml (2 tbsp)
175 g (6 oz)	plain flour	250 g (9 oz)
400 ml ($\frac{3}{4}$ pint)	milk	568 ml (1 pint)
pinch	salt	pinch
(Makes 8–10)		*(Makes 12–14)*

Mix the egg and oil into the flour with a spoon and beat in the milk. Add the salt and beat until smooth. Leave in the fridge for 30 minutes – longer won't hurt. Brush a small – 18-cm (7-in) – frying pan with oil and heat it until very hot, then pour in just enough batter to cover the base without holes. When it has set, shake it and turn over, or toss. I use a wide fish slice. Stack the pancakes between sheets of greaseproof paper.

FILLINGS
Palatschinken
15 ml (1 tbsp) each pancake, of apricot jam and toasted almonds – an Austrian recipe. Heat in the oven gently before serving.

Cheese and lemon
175 g (6 oz) each of caster sugar and cream cheese beaten together with the grated rind of a lemon. Heat gently. This makes enough for 10 pancakes. Use 225 g (8 oz) each sugar and cream cheese for 12–14 pancakes.

Grapes and honey

175 g (6 oz) seeded grapes mixed with 60 ml (4 tbsp) clear honey (for 10 pancakes) with a fresh orange quarter to squeeze over each pancake. Use 225 g (8 oz) seeded grapes and 90 ml (6 tbsp) honey for 12–14 pancakes.

CHOCOLATE GÂTEAU

A rich chocolate cake is always a favourite at any table. This one is layered with apricot and covered in fresh whipped cream, which makes it especially good for a party. It will keep for a week – without the cream of course.

Serves 4		Serves 6
175 g (6 oz)	plain flour	The same quantities
45 ml (3 level tbsp)	cocoa powder	as for 4 servings.
5 ml (1 level tsp)	baking powder	
5 ml (1 level tsp)	bicarbonate of soda	
150 g (5 oz)	caster sugar	
15 ml (1 level tbsp)	black treacle	
2	eggs, beaten	
150 ml ($\frac{1}{4}$ pint)	vegetable oil	
150 ml ($\frac{1}{4}$ pint)	milk	
	To finish	
100 g (4 oz)	apricot jam	
300 ml ($\frac{1}{2}$ pint)	whipping cream	

Mix all the dry ingredients. Add the wet ones and stir until well mixed. Pour into two 18-cm (7-in) greased cake tins and bake for 45 minutes at 170°C (325°F) mark 3. Turn out and cool on a rack. Spread one cake with apricot jam. Place the other on top and – just before serving – cover all over with whipped cream.

You can sprinkle grated chocolate on too if you like.

STRAWBERRY FOOL

One summer dish that neither I, my family or my friends ever seem to get tired of. When strawberries are newly in the shops, sugar and (if I'm feeling very self-indulgent) some cream to dip them in is all I want. But after the first flush I'm hooked on strawberry fool. Beware lest you become an addict too.

Serves 4		Serves 6
225 g (8 oz)	strawberries, hulled	350 g (12 oz)
100 g (4 oz)	caster sugar	175 g (6 oz)
300 ml ($\frac{1}{2}$ pint)	double cream	400 ml ($\frac{3}{4}$ pint)

Put the strawberries and sugar in a saucepan over a very gentle heat until the juice runs out of the strawberries, stirring only until all the sugar has dissolved and the whole mixture is scenting the air. Crush the fruit with a wooden spoon. Remove from the heat and cool. Whip the cream until thick, but not set hard, and stir carefully into the strawberry mixture. Pile it up into a white china dish and decorate with a few strawberry leaves, if you can get them. Chill for at least 1 hour. If you like your strawberry fool absolutely smooth, you can purée the strawberry mixture first in a blender before mixing it with the cream. But I like the texture that the strawberries – just crushed and still in little chunks – give the whole mixture.

MONT BLANC

This exotic pudding is named after its appearance – the famous mountain in the French Alps – a towering brown cone covered in snow. Equally imposing as a pudding, it's not nearly such a formidable task to make as to climb.

Serves 4		Serves 6
4	small meringue cases (about 6·5 cm ($2\frac{1}{2}$ in) in diameter)	6
300 ml ($\frac{1}{2}$ pint)	whipping cream	400 ml ($\frac{3}{4}$ pint)
450 g (1 lb)	sweetened chestnut purée	700 g ($1\frac{1}{2}$ lb)
15 ml (1 tbsp)	grated orange rind *or* chocolate	15 ml (1 tbsp)

You can make the meringue cases if you're an expert, but I usually buy mine from a good baker – white ones, not pink.

Beat the chestnut purée in a bowl, whip half the cream until thick, then fold the cream into the chestnut purée. Add the grated orange rind or chocolate and, dividing the mixture into 4 (6), pile it on to the meringue bases to form as tall peaks as possible. Chill until you are ready, and just before serving pour the rest of the cream over from the very top of each peak so that it runs down like snow.

BANANAS FOSTER

There's a famous restaurant in the old quarter of New Orleans in Louisiana called Brennan's. It's famous throughout America for its Sunday brunches and the highlight of these is always a dish invented at Brennan's called Bananas Foster. It's an education in how simple, everyday ingredients can be turned into something special with just a little knowledge and touch of flair.

Serves 4		Serves 6
4 large	bananas	6 large
100 g (4 oz)	butter	175 g (6 oz)
60 ml (4 level tbsp)	soft brown sugar	90 ml (6 level tbsp)
5 ml (1 level tsp)	ground cinnamon	5 ml (1 level tsp)
450 ml (17 fl oz)	vanilla ice cream	700 ml ($1\frac{1}{4}$ pint)

Peel the bananas, slice in half lengthways and cut each half in half again, giving you four long pieces per banana. Melt the butter in a large frying pan, add the sugar and stir until thoroughly dissolved and mixed. Add the bananas and roll over until they are thoroughly coated. Turn the heat down and cook gently for 3 minutes. Add the cinnamon and turn the heat up until the sugar and butter mixture starts to turn to toffee – about 1½ minutes. Pour immediately over the waiting ice cream making sure that each person gets a fair share of bananas. The mixture sets when it touches the ice cream, but remains hot and melting at the same time.

A taste sensation that just has to be experienced even if you can't make it to New Orleans.

PAVLOVA

Illustrated on the cover

An Australian dessert in origin, this fruit filled meringue was named after the famous ballet dancer for its lightness – as no doubt you will see when you taste it. It's much easier than it sounds.

Serves 4		Serves 6
3	egg whites	The same quantities
175 g (6 oz)	caster sugar	as for 4 servings.
2·5 ml (½ tsp)	vinegar	
2·5 ml (½ tsp)	vanilla essence	
1 punnet	strawberries *or*	
225 g (8 oz)	seeded or seedless grapes	
150 ml (¼ pint)	double cream	

Beat the egg whites until stiff, then add the sugar 15 ml (1 tbsp) at a time. When it is all in, add the vinegar and vanilla. It should be a glossy meringue. Grease a 20·5-cm (8-in) flan dish and pile the mixture in, scooping a dent in the middle. Put in a hot oven heated to 230°C (450°F) mark 8, turn down to 150°C (300°F) mark 2 for 30 minutes, then turn off for 1 hour. Remove and cool. Just before serving, fill with sliced or whole strawberries and cream – well whipped – or serve this separately.

The combination of flavours and textures is just fantastic.

WALNUT TREACLE TART

This is an adaptation of a traditional English recipe. The walnuts in it add a little crunch. It can be served warm or cold, but my preference is for warm, with a lot of pouring cream to go with it. About a million calories an ounce, and worth every one of them.

Serves 4		Serves 6
225 g (8 oz)	shortcrust pastry (home-made or packet)	the same quantities
100 g (4 oz)	butter	as for 4 servings.
50 g (2 oz)	sugar	
2	eggs, beaten	
175 g (6 oz)	golden syrup	
100 g (4 oz)	walnuts, finely chopped	
	grated rind of 1 lemon	
	juice of $\frac{1}{2}$ lemon	
pinch	salt	

Use the pastry to line a 21·5-cm (8½-in) tin with straight sides. Bake it in the oven for about 10 minutes at 200°C (400°F) mark 6 filled with some kitchen foil to stop it bubbling in the middle. Mix together the butter and sugar until they are smooth and beat in the eggs and syrup (warming it in a saucepan if it's too cold to pour). Add the walnuts, the grated rind and juice of the lemon and salt. Turn the mixture into the pastry case, having first removed the kitchen foil. Bake at 180°C (350°F) mark 4, for 45–55 minutes, until the top is brown, crispy and scented.

Try and let it cool enough not to burn your mouth! In fact, it tastes better eaten warm or cold.

FANCY FRUIT SALAD

The secret of a really good fruit salad is the syrup – easy to make, but making all the difference. It bathes the fruit while it's marinating, blending the flavours just enough, enhancing some and softening others so the whole becomes far more than just a mixture of fresh fruit. It's the perfect ending to a rich meal or dinner on a warm summer's night.

Serves 4		Serves 6
100 g (4 oz)	sugar	175 g (6 oz)
175 ml (6 fl oz)	water	300 ml ($\frac{1}{2}$ pint)
2	eating apples	3
1	melon	1
2	oranges	3
	and *either* a pomegranate *or* a punnet of strawberries	

The fruit can be varied as long as it's a mixture of crisp, scented, sharp and exotic. You can suit it to the season. Much more than four different sorts of fruit starts to become a little bit of a mess, so don't be tempted to add anything more than perhaps a few grapes.

Melt the sugar in a saucepan and let it start to go golden brown. Take if off the heat and carefully, so it doesn't splash you, pour in the water. Put back over the heat and mix until you have a pale golden caramel syrup. Let it cool. Core and thinly slice the apples but don't peel them. Seed the melon and cut into cubes off the skin. Peel the oranges and separate into segments, then cut each segment in half. Mix all the above fruit with the syrup and chill for at least 1 hour. Not more than 5 minutes before serving, scatter with the inside segments of the pomegranate or sliced strawberries. It looks really pretty in glass bowls. You can serve with cream if you like, but try at least to taste it without. The flavour is so distinctive you may not want to mask it.

HOT FRUIT SALAD

If you always thought fresh fruit had to be eaten cold this dish is going to be a revelation. It also has one of the most sensational appearances of all puddings. So if you're out to impress a little, this is the way to finish the meal.

Serves 4		Serves 6
1 medium	fresh pineapple, leaves still on	1 large
2	oranges	3
75 g (3 oz)	unsalted butter	100 g (4 oz)
30 ml (2 level tbsp)	granulated sugar	45 ml (3 level tbsp)
6	maraschino or glacé cherries	9

Begin by cutting the pineapple in half lengthways, so you have 2 boat-shaped pieces with the green leaves still on. Scoop out the flesh from the middle, leaving the outer shell intact. Put the pineapple boats on a serving tray as they are going to be the 'dishes' in which the pudding is served. Cut the pineapple flesh into 2·5-cm (1-in) cubes; peel the oranges, divide into segments and cut each in half. Melt the butter in a deep frying pan in which there's enough room for all the fruit. Do not let it brown. Add the pineapple and heat through, turning steadily; sprinkle with the sugar and orange pieces. Do not stir, but turn them all carefully so the fruit doesn't break but is heated right through. Pile it back into the shells, decorate with the cherries and serve *immediately*.

Hot it's sensational, cold it's not much fun. 'Oohs' and 'Aahs' will greet the appearance of this fruit salad that's tropical in more ways than one.

CHOCOLATE CHESTNUT MOULD

One of the grand desserts this – combining the richness of chocolate with the smoothness of puréed sweet chestnuts – and yet amazingly simple to do.

Serves 4		Serves 6
100 g (4 oz)	caster sugar	The same quantities
100 g (4 oz)	unsalted butter, softened	as for 4 servings.
175 g (6 oz)	plain chocolate	
440-g (15½-oz)	can unsweetened chestnut purée	
2·5 ml (½ tsp)	vanilla essence	

Cream the sugar and softened butter together in a bowl. Melt the chocolate slowly, keeping it smooth. Mix the chocolate, butter and sugar mixture, chestnut purée and vanilla essence together and beat until smooth. Put in a greased loaf tin and chill for at least 6 hours.

Turn out and decorate with crumbled chocolate flake or marrons glacés.

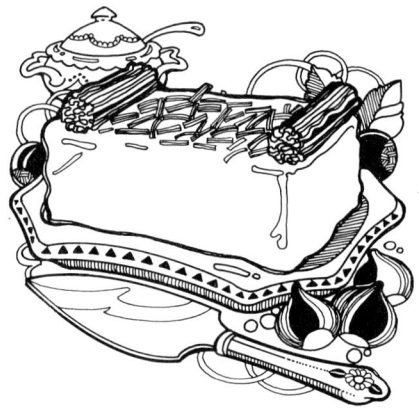

BERRY CREAM SPONGE

When strawberries are in season this makes a lovely easy pudding, but actually I think it's best with raspberries or blackberries. The slightly darker fruit with a sharper taste contrasts beautifully with the crisp, golden, sweet sponge and the lusciousness of the cream.

Serves 4		Serves 6
175 g (6 oz)	caster sugar	The same quantities
175 g (6 oz)	soft tub margarine	as for 4 servings.
3	eggs, beaten	
175 g (6 oz)	self raising flour	
5 ml (1 tsp)	vanilla essence	
300 ml (½ pint)	double cream	
225 g (8 oz)	strawberries, raspberries or blackberries	

Cream the sugar and margarine together until light and fluffy. Beat in the eggs, one at a time. Fold in the flour and vanilla essence. Pour into two 18-cm (7-in) greased sandwich tins (or use non-stick ones). Bake for 25 minutes at 190°C (375°F) mark 5 until risen and golden. Turn out and allow to cool on a wire rack. Beat the cream until thick, sweeten to taste (depending on berries used) with not more than 30 ml (2 level tbsp) sugar.

Spread half the cream on one cake, slice half the berries and lay them on top. Place the second cake on top, smooth side upwards. Spread the rest of the cream on top and decorate with the remaining berries.

The cake will keep for up to 2 hours in the fridge; after that the cream will start to collapse, so don't assemble it too soon.

PRALINE ICE CREAM

Home-made ice cream is really one of the great treats and this recipe, unlike most, requires neither an electric ice cream maker nor long complicated beatings while freezing. It's far too rich to develop those little spears of ice that often give away home-made ice creams.

Serves 4		Serves 6
15 ml (1 tbsp)	water	30 ml (2 tbsp)
50 g (2 oz)	granulated sugar	75 g (3 oz)
50 g (2 oz)	almonds	75 g (3 oz)
3	eggs	4
100 g (4 oz)	icing sugar	175 g (6 oz)
5 ml (1 tsp)	vanilla essence	7·5 ml (1½ tsp)
300 ml (½ pint)	double cream	400 ml (¾ pint)

Put the water and granulated sugar in a saucepan and heat, stirring until it caramelises and turns golden brown. Add the almonds and stir for 1 minute, then remove from the heat. Place the bottom of the pan in cold water, prise out the praline quickly and let it set hard on some greaseproof paper. (A non-stick pan is by far the best for this.) When cold, put the praline in a polythene bag and break it up with a rolling pin until it's a coarse powder. (You can also do this in the coffee-grinder bit of a blender.)

To make the ice cream, beat the eggs and the icing sugar together until they are doubled in volume. Add the vanilla. In a separate bowl beat the cream until it's thick but not whipped. Mix it with the praline and add to the egg and sugar mixture. Stir until thoroughly mixed, put in a polythene container and freeze in the freezer compartment of your refrigerator set to maximum or in a freezer. It will take about 2 hours to freeze and should be taken out and put into the ordinary refrigerator half an hour before serving. I like putting it into tall wine glasses which have also been chilled in the fridge.

You may think it's the first real ice cream you've ever tasted.

MARMALADE ICE CREAM

Using the same method as for the Praline ice cream recipe, you can make delicious bitter orange ice cream with 60–90 ml (4–6 tbsp) of marmalade instead of the praline. Otherwise follow the above recipe exactly, adding the marmalade (with any extra large segments of peel cut up with scissors) when you would add the almond and sugar mixture. Any kind of marmalade will do except jelly marmalades, because the peel gives it texture. I've even been known to use ginger marmalade on occasions, for a really surprising flavour.

FRENCH APPLE FLAN

This is one of those very simple open pies which are the foundation of the French reputation for wonderful food. It'll keep for more than a day ahead, and in the unlikely event of having any left over it goes only too well with coffee at elevenses.

Serves 4		Serves 6
225 g (8 oz)	shortcrust pastry	The same quantities
450 g (1 lb)	eating apples	as for 4 servings.
100 g (4 oz)	apricot jam	
45 ml (3 level tbsp)	icing sugar	
5 ml (1 level tsp)	ground cinnamon	

Roll out the pastry and use to line a 20·5-cm (8-in) fluted or loose-bottomed flan dish. (The china ones are very pretty but they are much harder to serve from.) Bake the pastry blind (i.e. without any filling) at 200°C (400°F) mark 6 for 10 minutes, with a large sheet of crumpled foil in the middle of it to prevent it blistering.

Peel and slice the apples to look like orange segments. Spread 15 ml (1 level tbsp) of the jam on the pastry case when it's cooled a little. Arrange the apple slices around the case in concentric rings. Sprinkle on the icing sugar and cinnamon and put it back in the oven for 10 minutes. Melt the remaining jam with 30 ml (2 tbsp) of water. Pour it over the tart and let it set for at least 5 minutes. You eat it warm (not hot), or cold.

If it's warm, pouring cream's best. If it's cold, whipped cream makes it absolutely luxurious.

CHOCOLATE MOUSSE

This must be one of the all-time favourite puddings with everybody, and yet it's probably one of the easiest ever to make.

Serves 4		Serves 6
100 g (4 oz)	plain chocolate	175 g (6 oz)
60 ml (4 tbsp)	orange squash (not juice)	90 ml (6 tbsp)
50 g (2 oz)	unsalted butter	75 g (3 oz)
4	eggs	6
	grated rind of 1 orange	

Melt the chocolate in the orange squash very gently over a low heat. When it's melted, add the butter and beat until smooth. Separate the eggs and, off the heat, beat in the egg yolks until the chocolate mixture is smooth. Let it cool while you beat the egg whites until they are really stiff, then fold into the chocolate mixture with the orange rind. Put it into small custard cups or one large mould and chill it for at least 2 hours. You can add grated chocolate or crystallised ginger on the top.

Serve with little crisp almondy biscuits.

CHEESECAKE

Both the Americans and the Italians lay claim to this recipe. I'm not convinced by either argument myself, but I must admit that my adaptation has slightly more of the American than the Italian style about it. Either way, it's a lovely sumptuous way to end a meal that hasn't had any cheese in it already.

Serves 4		Serves 6
175 g (6 oz)	digestive biscuits	The same quantities
75 g (3 oz)	butter	as for 4 servings.
2·5 ml ($\frac{1}{2}$ level tsp)	ground cinnamon (optional)	
225 g (8 oz)	'Philadelphia' *or* other cream cheese	
300 ml ($\frac{1}{2}$ pint)	soured cream	
60 ml (4 level tbsp)	caster sugar	
	grated rind and juice of 1 lemon	
225 g (8 oz)	black cherry jam	

Break up the biscuits until they are fairly fine crumbs. (Use a blender or a polythene bag and a rolling pin to do this.) Melt the butter and mix thoroughly with the crumbs. Add the cinnamon at this stage if you like it. Put the mixture into a 20·5-cm (8-in) pie dish and, using your knuckles and your hand, spread it quickly all over the pie dish to form an even coating. As it cools it sets, and forms a lovely crunchy crust for the filling.

For the filling, beat the cheese with half the soured cream, add the caster sugar and the rind and juice of the lemon, beat until smooth and pour into the crust. Spread evenly, beat the remaining soured cream until smooth, pour over the top, and place in the fridge to set.

Melt the jam over a very gentle heat. Remove the cheesecake from the refrigerator and pour the cooled jam carefully over it. Smooth over so that it forms an even coating. Put the cake back in the fridge for at least 1 more hour. Serve cut in wedges.

YOGURT CRUNCH

Health foods are very much a part of our lives these days. There's muesli often replacing cornflakes on the breakfast table, and yogurt, unheard of 15 years ago, taken for granted. This dish is an almost shamefully easy way of using two of the most common health foods to make a really delicious and extremely virtuous pudding. Although anything that tastes this good can't be all good for you, can it?

Serves 4		Serves 6
600 ml (1 pint)	natural yogurt	900 ml (1½ pints)
225 g (8 oz)	white grapes (seeded or seedless)	350 g (12 oz)
75 g (3 oz)	honey muesli*	100 g (4 oz)

Mix the yogurt and grapes, cut in half (whether or not they're seedless). If you have a very sweet tooth, you can add a little sugar at this stage, but I think it unnecessary. Pile into wine glasses and spoon on to the top of each 30 ml (2 level tbsp) of the honey muesli. Stir gently, leaving enough to coat the top of the yogurt in each glass. Chill in the fridge for 1 hour.

Crunchy, sharp and sweet, it's most refreshing after a rich meal or a dinner party in the summer.

*This is sold under various names, like 'original crunchy' and 'honey crunch'. It is *not* ordinary muesli but the one that has been baked to get a particularly crisp outside.

The Cheese Course

French tradition has it that you serve the cheese course (and in France tradition usually *does* have it) immediately after the main course, and *follow* it with a sweet. British habits, however, have usually dictated that you eat the cheese after the pudding. I must admit I've never really understood this last one, because I prefer to get up from the table having finished with something light, clean and preferably a little sweet on the palate. However, you must do whatever suits you best. What the addition of a cheese course does do, is turn a simple three course meal into the beginnings of a fairly grand four or even five course one.

Whichever way you play it, there are a few simple rules about serving cheese. Firstly, don't serve more than three kinds at a time unless you are a real expert. The correct way to do it is to have a mild, a medium and a strong cheese, preferably varying in their texture; thus a creamy one, a firm one and perhaps a crumbly one can mix and match with the strength of flavour any way you like. A good French combination for example, might be Brie (very mild and creamy), a Pont L'Évêque (which is firm and slightly more tangy) and a Bresse Bleu (which is the French answer to Stilton, crumbly and very strong). A British combination might be Caerphilly (mild and very crumbly), Wensleydale (firm and sharp) and perhaps some Ilchester, a recently developed, manufactured British cheese, rather like a creamy Cheshire, flavoured with garlic and wild herbs.

The choice is up to you, and you can manage with one good piece of cheese on its own, if you like. The important thing is that it should be good, not plastic wrapped, and preferably cut in your presence off the whole cheese and kept out of the fridge – and out of polythene bags, if possible, until you come to eat it.

When you're eating cheese very much on its own like this, as a course in a meal, there are again two ways of handling it. The French way is with a knife and fork as though it were a piece of steak. The English way, which in this case I much prefer, is with a number of accompaniments, some of which are more traditional than others. I'm not particularly fond of biscuits with cheese, unless they happen to be wheatmeal or not-too-sweet digestives. My personal bent is for some crisp French bread that's recently been heated in the oven to make sure the crust is as crunchy as possible, a generous dish of golden, salted butter, some chunks of crisp celery (the heart bits are quite the nicest), and, if you happen to be that way inclined, some suitable dried fruit – fresh dried figs in the winter, dried pears or apricots. If you want to be really exotic, search for some of those special dried fruit-cheeses that come from southern Europe and the Mediterranean. There are ones made of apricots, quinces and apples. They are not always easy to find, but are incredibly delicious, especially with the milder, creamier cheeses and some of that crisp bread I was mentioning.

Whatever accompaniments you choose to

serve, remember that by now your guests are pretty well fed, or at least ought to be, so the cheese is really a finishing touch to the meal, not a major contributor in itself to nourishment or fullness. That doesn't mean don't bother, it just means don't spend too much money, time or effort compared to the rest of the meal, on the cheese board, unless of course, you're not going to serve any pudding. If that's the case, then have a generous cheese board with a small basket of fruit – apples, pears and grapes always seem to me to go best with cheese. It is a perfect solution, and also very labour and time saving. There is, by the way, a lovely device on the market, which looks like a spoked wheel. Pressed down over an apple or a pear, it cores it and simultaneously cuts the remaining flesh into twelve neat segments which can be picked off and eaten without any nasty mess or effort. If you can find one of these, it's a nice idea to do an apple or a pear at a time and pass it round the table for people to help themselves.

If you don't usually serve cheese, try including a cheese course in your next dinner party. You'll be surprised how well it's received. It has one other advantage, in that it gives you a break, because the cheese course and all that goes with it can be laid in the dining room long before the meal starts (cheese covered with a little cling film – not sealed down, but just to keep the moisture from evaporating too quickly). All you have to do is put it on the table when the main course is over and before you produce the pud.

Five Party Menus

Fondue for ten

There are a number of kinds of dishes served under the title 'fondue'. What they all share is being cooked at the table over a spirit burner in a saucepan or casserole. There are fondues with chunks of beef, even sweet fondues with a chocolate sauce, but the best of all, and without doubt one of the greatest ice breakers at any party, is the Swiss fondue made with cheese.

Guests are given long forks and chunks of crusty French bread or crisp pieces of baby vegetables to dip in a bubbling, golden, tangy cheese sauce. As each piece is coated, they pop it in their mouths and begin again. The taste is terrific, the effort minimal, and the fun of doing it yourself in a group quickly gets people talking and enjoying themselves together. There's an old Swiss tradition that if anybody loses a piece of bread in the cheese saucepan when he's dunking it, a man has to buy a round of drinks and a woman has to give every man in the room a kiss. My own view is that in these liberated days, the kissing forfeit should apply to men as well – though I doubt if you will persuade many of the women to buy a round of drinks!

This recipe serves eight to ten people very adequately and you don't need a lot afterwards. If I'm serving anything at all, I usually follow the fondue with a crisp, finely chopped salad (using Iceberg or cos lettuce) and one of the fruit sweets, according to the time of year. Although the Swiss usually eat this dish in the winter, it has the advantage, when served with the right dipping ingredients, of being light enough for a summer evening meal as well.

FONDUE

300 ml ($\frac{1}{2}$ pint) apple juice
350 g (12 oz) Gruyère cheese
350 g (12 oz) Emmenthal cheese
15 ml (1 tbsp) lemon juice
5 ml (1 level tsp) garlic salt
120 ml (8 tbsp) milk
15 ml (1 level tbsp) cornflour
1 French loaf cut into 2·5-cm (1-in) cubes
   and/or
small cauliflower florets
1-cm ($\frac{1}{2}$-in) apple cubes
1-cm ($\frac{1}{2}$-in) cucumber cubes
button mushrooms

To make this dish, ideally you need a fondue set. But an ordinary saucepan will do, keeping it hot at the table on either a portable ring or burner. (If necessary, you can use a heated serving tray.) On the cooker to begin with, heat the apple juice and bring to boiling point. Grate the cheese finely and add it with the lemon juice and garlic salt to the apple juice, stirring until all the cheese is melted. Mix the milk and cornflour, add and stir until the mixture comes to just below the boil again and thickens. Put the saucepan on the fondue burner or heated ring, set so that it just bubbles. Have some long forks ready – there are special fondue forks on the market if you can find them – then serve with the bread and/or crispy vegetables. Even if you are specialising on the vegetables there should be some bread available at the table.

Remember when you are dunking to get your cube right down to the bottom of the sauce where some of the more tasty morsels of cheese are to be found.

Barbecue for twelve

A lot of people I know have a horror of barbecues – burnt food, smoke-smelling hair and clothes, and tomato ketchup over everything from the begonias to little Billy's dungarees. But have courage – it can be done both easily and elegantly. And if the weather's too bad, you can always bring this party indoors and cook in the oven and on the grill. It isn't quite the same as watching the sun go down from your own patio, or the deck of your own yacht, but it'll still taste good and give a hint of the flavour of the great outdoors. This menu is almost infinitely stretchable if you've got a big enough barbecue. The quantities I'm giving are for twelve people with hearty appetites.

When it comes to equipment, I've known people get some of the best results from a square of bricks with one side removed to provide a draught and chicken wire over the top as a grill. But, both for appearance and safety's sake, I would suggest one of the Japanese cast iron barbecues that come in various sizes and shapes, and allow both for solidity and safety and a fairly fine judgment as to how close to keep your fire to the food.

For any barbecuing, make sure: that the apparatus is not likely to get knocked over or bumped into, especially by children; that you've got something nearby to put out the fire quickly should you need to; that you've got tools long enough to allow you to handle the food on the barbecue without burning yourself in the process. And, especially, if you're doing it in the late evening, you've got enough light to see what you're doing without having to hold a torch in your teeth while you turn the chicken over. The worst singeing I ever gave food was when trying to barbecue in the pitch dark on a tropical island using my sense of smell and a waning moon.

Begin by making the basic barbecue sauce.

BARBECUE SAUCE

1 large onion, skinned and finely chopped
30 ml (2 tbsp) cooking oil
454-g (1-lb) can tomato paste
60 ml (4 level tbsp) soft brown sugar
60 ml (4 tbsp) vinegar
15 ml (1 level tbsp) garlic salt
30 ml (2 level tbsp) prepared mustard
30 ml (2 tbsp) Worcestershire sauce

Fry the onion in the oil until soft but not brown. Add all the other ingredients. Stir until they are well combined and simmer, uncovered, for at least 10 minutes. Use this mixture to brush all the food you are cooking on the barbecue. Heat it up in a pan, on the corner of the grill, to serve with the food when it's cooked.

Barbecued meat
You can use almost any quickly cooked meat to serve on a barbecue. My favourites are chicken pieces and kebabs. They are easy to handle, cook quickly and take particularly well to the slightly smoky flavour that cooking over charcoal gives.

Before you start to cook, make sure that the barbecue has been alight for at least half an hour, that there are no flames from the charcoal and that it has a smooth covering of grey ash. It may look less hot than when it was flaming but the heat's right there where you need it.

BARBECUED CHICKEN

Brush 12 chicken pieces with the Barbecue sauce. Place them on the pre-heated grill close to the charcoal. Grill for 10 minutes. Turn over, remove one notch further away from the heat and grill for a further 8–10 minutes, depending on the thickness of the chicken. Just before serving, brush one more time with the Barbecue sauce.

BEEF KEBABS

1·4 kg (3 lb) topside, cut into 1-cm ($\frac{1}{2}$-in) cubes
90 ml (6 tbsp) soy sauce
5 ml (1 level tsp) garlic salt
5 ml (1 level tsp) brown sugar

Put the beef cubes into a marinade made from all the other ingredients and leave to stand for at least 1–2 hours. Thread them on to skewers (preferably flat-sided skewers to facilitate turning them over during the cooking process). Don't put more than 6 cubes on each skewer, but pack them close together. Grill them close to the heat for 6 minutes a side. You can mix the marinade into some of the Barbecue sauce afterwards, heated through to make an accompanying sauce.

Have two salads ready in advance. My favourites are Potato salad and Coleslaw.

POTATO SALAD

1·4 kg (3 lb) new potatoes
60 ml (4 tbsp) vinegar
10 ml (2 level tsp) sea salt
300 ml ($\frac{1}{2}$ pint) mayonnaise (see page 40 *or*
  use Hellmann's)
1 bunch spring onions, trimmed

Boil the washed but unpeeled new potatoes until just cooked. (Avoid getting them over-cooked or soggy.) Cut them in half or, if very large, into quarters. While still warm, pour over the vinegar and sprinkle on the salt. Allow to cool. Add the mayonnaise and the spring onions (white and green parts), cut into 0·5-cm ($\frac{1}{4}$-in) lengths. Toss the lot together, place in a bowl and leave in the fridge for at least 1 hour before serving.

COLESLAW

900 g (2 lb) white cabbage heart (Dutch-style
  cabbage)
225 g (8 oz) carrots, peeled
225 g (8 oz) eating apples, cored
226-g (8-oz) can pineapple bits, drained

For the dressing
150 ml ($\frac{1}{4}$ pint) salad oil
75 ml (5 tbsp) lemon juice
2·5 ml ($\frac{1}{2}$ level tsp) salt
5 ml (1 level tsp) sugar
10 ml (2 level tsp) prepared French mustard

Shred the cabbage as finely as possible, removing any discoloured outer leaves and the hard heart. Grate the carrots and the unpeeled apples. Mix all the fruit and vegetables together, tossing to make sure they are blended. Make a dressing with the oil, lemon juice, salt, sugar and mustard. If you have a blender, whip it in this until thick and creamy ; otherwise a good shaking or beating with a whisk will do. Pour over the salad, turn to mix thoroughly, and leave for half an hour for the flavours to blend.

BARBECUED BANANAS

Here's an unusual barbecue pudding to finish this meal with – if you still have room.

1 banana per person
5 ml (1 tsp) lemon juice per person
5 ml (1 level tsp) soft brown sugar per
  person

Without breaking the banana, peel back a strip of skin so that you have a canoe with the banana still in it. Sprinkle the lemon juice and then sugar along the open side. Replace the skin loosely and wrap in foil. Bake the bananas in your oven at 180°C (350°F) mark 4 for 20 minutes and then turn the oven down to keep them warm. After all the meat's been cooked on the barbecue, add the bananas to heat through. Serve with lashings of cream.

If you don't believe hot bananas can taste good, just try these.

An Indian feast for six

Indian food, although everybody seems to like to eat it, is very much a cooking mystery to most people. I hope this menu, designed to feed six people exotically but craftily, will dispel any fears you may have. Another fear to dispel is the worry that the house will smell of curry for days afterwards. It's simply not true if you follow the methods given below.

This menu comes from northern India, where much of the food is more delicately spiced and less loaded with chilli than we have often come to believe has to be the case with Indian food. The normal way of serving is to put all the dishes on the table at once and let guests help themselves to the varieties. If you want to be terribly authentic and yet extremely crafty, buy six chapatis (flat unleavened bread) from your local Indian take-away shop, heat them through in the oven, and serve with the rest of the meal. It's not essential, but it does add an authentic touch.

The basis of the meal is a pilau – a rice dish spiced to give it a little extra kick.

PILAU

50 g (2 oz) butter
350 g (12 oz) basmati *or* patna long grain rice
piece of cinnamon stick
1 bay leaf
5 ml (1 level tsp) salt
700 ml (1¼ pints) chicken stock (a stock cube
  will do for this)

In a big saucepan, melt the butter, add the rice and fry gently for about 5 minutes, until it glistens and goes a little transparent. Add the cinnamon stick, bay leaf, salt and, all at once, the chicken stock. Stir until thoroughly mixed. Bring to the boil, turn down and simmer with a lid on over a very low heat for 25 minutes. At the end of that time the rice should have absorbed all the chicken stock, and be fragrant with the cinnamon and bay leaf. Switch the heat off and stretch a tea towel over the pan – the pilau will keep warm, fluffy and dry for at least another 20 minutes without further cooking.

CHICKEN TIKKA

This is a kind of home-made Tandoori chicken. Very easy to do, and absolutely delicious.

6 chicken portions, boned if possible and
  skinned
1 medium onion, skinned and sliced
150 ml (¼ pint) natural yogurt
30 ml (2 level tbsp) Tandoori mix *or* curry
  powder
5 ml (1 level tsp) garlic salt

Cut 2 or 3 long gashes down to the bone in the chicken portions, to allow the marinade to penetrate. Mix all the other ingredients together and cover the chicken with it, spooning well over. Marinate for at least 2 hours. Even up to 12 hours won't hurt as the longer you leave it, the better the flavour penetrates the chicken.

Twenty minutes before you are ready to cook, heat the oven up to 230°C (450°F) mark 8. Put the chicken on a wire grid, in a roasting tin to catch the drips. It must bake in the dry, not in its own juices. Bake for 25 minutes. Turn it, then cook for another 5 minutes. The outside should be crisp and crunchy, the inside moist and succulent.

If you can't bear to waste the marinade, bring it to the boil on top of the cooker, simmer gently for 2–3 minutes and serve as a sauce with, not over, the chicken.

KEEMA AND PEAS

One of the most simple and delicious of traditional curries.

450 g (1 lb) minced lamb (beef will do, lamb is better)
30 ml (2 level tbsp) mild curry powder or Kashmiri curry paste
1 large onion, skinned and chopped
1 clove of garlic, skinned and crushed
400 ml (¾ pint) beef stock
100 g (4 oz) frozen peas
15 ml (1 tbsp) lemon juice
30 ml (2 level tbsp) tomato paste
10 ml (2 level tsp) salt
freshly ground black pepper

Fry the minced meat in its own fat until it browns and separates into crumbs. Add the curry powder or paste (do use a mild one unless you like your eyes watering). Fry gently with the meat for about 3 minutes. Add the onion and crushed garlic and turn again for 1 minute. Add the stock and let the mixture simmer gently for 20 minutes. At this point you can leave it until you are almost ready to serve – up to 6 hours later. Just before serving, bring back to the boil, add the peas (frozen are fine), the lemon juice, tomato paste and seasoning. Stir until the peas are just cooked and the mixture is smooth and glistening.

DHAL

This is a traditional Indian accompaniment to most meals. It can be made in a variety of ways: I happen to be very fond of this version. It's so good it's almost worth eating on its own with a little dish of yogurt and cucumber, and some mango chutney. Those, by the way, are the right accompaniments to the whole meal – just slice the cucumber finely into 150 ml (¼ pint) yogurt, and buy some of the best looking mango chutney you can find.

225 g (8 oz) lentils (red or golden ones are the best)
600 ml (1 pint) water
5 ml (1 level tsp) salt
5 ml (1 level tsp) turmeric
pinch chilli powder

Wash the lentils and put them in a saucepan. Cover with the water. Add the salt, turmeric and chilli powder and bring to the boil. Turn down and simmer gently until the liquid has almost all been absorbed and the lentils have formed a creamy purée. This should take, depending upon the size of the lentils, between 35–50 minutes. Once again, Dhal can be made in advance, and reheated, with advantage. The flavour seems to get better, not worse. If it gets too thick, add a little more water and stir.

For a pudding I can think of nothing better than Mango fool (see page 66). To drink with your Indian feast, serve lemonade, lager, or just plain water.

A posh buffet for forty

Here is a buffet suitable for a grand celebration; the numbers are adjustable. On the menu we have:

WATERCRESS SOUP
SAUMON VERT
CELEBRATION CHICKEN
RICE SALAD
SALAD ELANA
CHOCOLATE GÂTEAU (SEE PAGE 68)

This menu has the hot dish (that I think ought to be included in every buffet) at the beginning. It has two main courses, one fish, one chicken, that both look incredibly attractive, and appeal to everybody. The salmon, 're-scaled', after it's been cooked, with delicate slices of cucumber, looks most striking as a centrepiece. And the subtly spiced chicken is a favourite with absolutely everybody. It's an adaptation of a recipe devised for the banquet at the Queen's Coronation, where every taste had to be catered for.

The salads are refreshingly different – Salad Elana with its mixture of strawberries and cucumber (just wait until you taste it) and the equally exotic Rice salad, with pineapple and peppers.

WATERCRESS SOUP

12 bunches watercress, trimmed
12 Spanish onions, skinned
4·5 kg (10 lb) potatoes, peeled
900 g (2 lb) butter
8·5 litres (15 pints) light chicken stock (see Celebration chicken recipe)
salt and freshly ground pepper
1·1 litres (2 pints) single cream

To begin with you need a saucepan (or 2 sauce-pans) large enough to take the whole mixture, which will come to nearly 13·5 litres (3 gallons) capacity when cooking.

Wash the watercress carefully, making sure no rubber bands or yellow bits are left. Set aside 2 bunches for garnish. Chop the rest together with the onions and the potatoes, making sure that the bits are fairly fine. The mixture can be processed in a food mixer. Melt the butter, add the chopped vegetables and stir until coated. Add the chicken stock, bring to the boil and simmer for 45 minutes, until the potato is completely dissolved into the soup, as a purée. Stir vigorously, using a beater if possible. Season and, just before serving, add all the single cream, mixing 600 ml (1 pint) thoroughly, and swirling the other on top of the soup to produce a marbled effect. The juice of 2 or 3 lemons can be added if the soup is to be kept warm for a very long time before adding the cream.

Garnish with the reserved watercress leaves.

SAUMON VERT

1 whole salmon – 1·8–2·3 kg (4–5 lb)
2 lemons
bouquet garni (celery sprig, thyme sprig, parsley sprig, piece of lemon peel)
5 ml (1 level tsp) peppercorns
2 cucumbers

For the mayonnaise
4 eggs
300 ml ($\frac{1}{2}$ pint) olive oil
300 ml ($\frac{1}{2}$ pint) sunflower oil
90 ml (6 tbsp) lemon juice
30 ml (2 level tbsp) Dijon mustard
20 ml (4 level tsp) salt
20 ml (4 level tsp) sugar
freshly ground pepper

Put the fish either in a fish kettle large enough to take it, or wrap it carefully in well buttered foil. In the fish kettle, cover it with cold water, add the juice of the lemons, the bouquet garni and peppercorns, bring to the boil, *simmer* for 4 minutes only, cover, switch off and leave to cool in its own liquid. Surprisingly, it will cook through in this time.

If using foil, slice the lemons and lay them on both sides of the fish, squeezing the tag ends of the lemons over. Seal the foil carefully without pressing it down on to the fish, and bake at 180°C (350°F) mark 4, for 10 minutes per 450 g (1 lb). Remove from the oven and allow to cool without opening the foil.

When the fish is cold, skin it very carefully (the skin should come away without any difficulty), and lay it on a serving dish. Score the cucumbers all round lengthways with a fork to produce ridges. Slice them wafer thin and use the best slices to overlap down and along the salmon to

84

recreate fish scales. The frilly effect on the edge of the cucumber makes a marvellous pattern. Use the rest of the cucumber slices in overlapping rows around the dish, both to decorate it and to be eaten later.

Make Blender mayonnaise, using half the ingredients at a time, and following the technique described on page 40. Serve the mayonnaise in a big bowl next to the salmon.

CELEBRATION CHICKEN

7 roasting chickens
75 g (3 oz) butter
75 ml (5 level tbsp) curry powder
2·3 litres (4 pints) milk
90 ml (6 level tbsp) flour
salt
two 340-g (12-oz) jars mango chutney
300 ml ($\frac{1}{2}$ pint) lemon juice
600 ml (1 pint) double cream
parsley sprigs and lettuce to garnish

Poach the chickens in water to cover for 45–60 minutes (the stock is perfect for the Watercress soup). Skin the chickens and cut into neat portions, removing the bones. Put the chicken portions on large oval serving dishes. Melt the butter and add the curry powder. Fry gently for 2 minutes. Add the milk and whisk in the flour. (This is possibly best done in 2 batches, using half the ingredients in each.) Bring to the boil whisking regularly until thick and creamy. Simmer for 5 minutes. Season with salt at this point – quite generously. Allow to cool a little, add the chutney (cutting up any large pieces of mango) and stir in the lemon juice. Whip the cream until thick but not stiff, and add that too. Pour the sauce over the chicken pieces.

This dish will keep in the fridge for up to 3 hours after it's been made, but shouldn't be kept waiting much longer. If you want to prepare it well in advance, store the chicken pieces and dressing separately in the fridge, well covered. Pour the dressing over just before serving.

Decorate, if possible, with pieces of fresh mango or if not, with sprigs of parsley and small golden lettuce leaves.

RICE SALAD

1·4 kg (3 lb) basmati *or* long grain rice
15 ml (1 level tbsp) salt
three 450-g (1-lb) bags frozen exotic mixed vegetables (including peppers)
2 heads celery, washed and chopped
two 566-g (1 lb 4-oz) cans pineapple chunks, drained and cut into quarters

For the dressing
600 ml (1 pint) salad oil
200 ml (7 fl oz) lemon juice
15 ml (1 level tbsp) salt
30 ml (2 level tbsp) sugar

Put the rice into saucepans with enough cold water to cover by at least 12·5 cm (5 in). Add the salt, bring to the boil and simmer for 12 minutes. Drain in a sieve and, while still warm, add the dressing made from the oil, lemon juice, salt and sugar mixed together thoroughly. (A blender is a good idea for mixing in these quantities.) Cool.

Simmer the frozen vegetables for 5 minutes in a little salted water. Drain well. Add the vegetables with the celery and pineapple to the rice. Toss the whole salad and refrigerate for at least 2 hours to allow the flavours to mix.

SALAD ELANA

10 punnets strawberries, hulled
5 cucumbers
freshly ground black pepper
1 litre (1$\frac{3}{4}$ pints) fresh orange juice
300 ml ($\frac{1}{2}$ pint) salad oil

Wash and slice the strawberries. Cut the cucumbers in half lengthways, scoop out the seeds with a strong teaspoon and cut each length into very thin half-moon shaped slices. Arrange these around the dish in overlapping layers with strawberry slices alternating with cucumber, finishing with strawberry slices. Season generously with black pepper. Mix the orange juice and oil, and dress not more than 30 minutes before serving.

To prepare well in advance, assemble the salad and cover with cling film. Store the prepared dressing in a covered container in the fridge and pour over just before serving.

Cheap and cheerful buffet for twenty

Here is a smaller and more homely buffet. The menu is:

CORNY TOMATOES

CHILLI CON CARNE

MEXICAN RICE

AVOCADO PURÉE

FRESH FRUIT SALAD (SEE PAGE 71)

CORNY TOMATOES

20 large fresh tomatoes
salt and freshly ground pepper
four 326-g (11½-oz) cans sweetcorn kernels, drained
700 g (1½ lb) cottage cheese
chopped parsley

For the dressing
300 ml (½ pint) salad oil
150 ml (¼ pint) lemon juice
5 ml (1 level tsp) salt
5 ml (1 level tsp) sugar
15 ml (1 level tbsp) grainy French mustard

Cut 'lids' off the tomatoes and scoop out the insides leaving the shells intact (do not waste the insides, they will go into the Chilli con carne). Salt them lightly and leave them upside down to drain for at least 20 minutes. Mix the sweetcorn and cottage cheese together. Season with salt and pepper. Pack into the tomato shells. Sprinkle the parsley over the top of each shell.

Blend the salad dressing ingredients together and just before serving pour 15 ml (1 tbsp) of dressing into each tomato.

CHILLI CON CARNE

2·3 kg (5 lb) minced beef
90 ml (6 tbsp) vegetable oil
10 ml (2 level tsp) chilli powder
1·4 kg (3 lb) Spanish onions, skinned and chopped
15 ml (1 level tbsp) ground cumin
two 800-g (28-oz) cans Italian tomatoes (*or* 1 can plus the insides from 20 tomatoes – see Corny tomatoes above)
454-g (1-lb) can tomato paste
five 454-g (1-lb) cans red kidney beans
15 ml (1 level tbsp) ground cinnamon
salt and freshly ground pepper

Fry the beef in the oil until well browned but in separate grains. Add the chilli powder and then the onion. Turn until they are all well coated in oil. Add the cumin and stir well. Add the tomatoes, tomato paste, beans and enough liquid to make the mixture moist but not runny (this will depend on the size of pan or pans you cook it in). Add the cinnamon and seasoning, bring to the boil and simmer for at least 1½ hours; 2 hours will not hurt it. Stir occasionally and add more water if the mixture becomes too thick to stir easily.

MEXICAN RICE

1·4 kg (3 lb) long grain rice
4 red *or* green peppers, seeded and chopped
2 large bunches spring onions, trimmed and chopped
1·1 litres (2 pints) tomato juice
1·7 litres (3 pints) water
salt and freshly ground pepper

Mix the rice, peppers, the white parts of the spring onions, tomato juice and water together. Season generously with salt and pepper. Bring to the boil and simmer for approximately 15–20 minutes, until all the liquid has been absorbed. Stir and serve with the green parts of the spring onions finely chopped and sprinkled over it.

AVOCADO PURÉE

6–8 ripe avocados (depending on size)
300 ml (½ pint) undiluted lime juice cordial
150 ml (¼ pint) salad oil
600 ml (1 pint) mayonnaise, home-made (page 40) *or* Hellmann's
salt and freshly ground pepper
2 large cos lettuces, washed

Halve the avocados lengthways, remove the stones and scoop out the flesh. Place it in a blender with the lime juice and oil and blend until smooth. Add the mayonnaise and mix thoroughly. Check the seasoning. Serve in a bowl lined with lettuce leaves that can be used as long spoons – each lettuce leaf bringing with it a spoonful of avocado purée to cool the spiciness of the Chilli con carne.

A large fruit salad is probably the best pudding to follow this filling but unusual buffet meal.

What to Drink with the Meal

The first thing to remember when choosing what to drink with your meal is not to be intimidated. If you don't like wine, then don't drink wine, drink fruit juice or Perrier water instead. If you like sweet wine, then drink sweet wine. There are no rules except for the wine snobs. There are only guidelines, and the object of the exercise is, you may remember, that everybody should enjoy themselves. The important thing is to make sure that your guests and your family arrive at the table in a fit state to enjoy the meal and are able to get up and leave afterwards in the same condition.

If you do want to serve alcohol with the meal, wine is of course the traditional drink. But it's worth remembering that it's best avoided where really strong flavoured food (like Indian curries), or exotic tastes (like some Chinese food) are concerned. It's also not a good idea to serve it where there is an extremely sharp or acid flavour such as lemon juice, oranges or a vinaigrette sauce around. You can safely ignore that rule where a salad is part of a meal, but ignore it at your own, and the wine's, peril otherwise. With strong and spicy food, something with a touch of sweetness in it, whether lemonade or European-style lager beer is usually most acceptable. Either way it needs to be served cold.

With wine itself, the basic rule is that 'like goes with like'. With red meat – beef, lamb, game – you serve a red wine; with white foods – fish, chicken, eggs – you serve a white wine. (The table at the end of this section lists some types of wine, and examples of these types to look for, related to the type of food with which they are traditionally served.) But this rule is not engraved in stone. Even in very posh circles it's quite acceptable to serve, for example, a fruity German Hock with a steak that's been cooked in peppercorns and a mustard sauce. So, in the last resort you must suit yourself and your own palate. Generally however, with savoury foods, the wine drunk is dry or medium dry and not sweet.

If you're feeling like splashing out, and drinking Champagne, it's quite right and proper to drink it all the way through the meal from beginning to end, regardless of what you are eating (curry is still an exception in this case of course). If you like, you can start a meal with Champagne, especially if you are using one of the fancier starters, and switch to the appropriate colour of still wine when you reach the main course.

If you want to serve cheese at the end of the meal, make sure that you have enough wine left to provide a glass to go with it. For the sweet course, if you want to go on serving wine it's best to buy half a bottle of sweet wine, either red or white; these usually come from the more southern parts of Europe. It's also an opportunity, if you haven't been serving sparkling wine before, to serve Asti Spumante, an Italian sparkling wine with an extraordinary fruity, grapey taste that goes well with most puddings.

In terms of quantity, allow about half a bottle a person for moderate drinkers. A litre bottle should see four people quite well through a meal. Beware of opening a second one at the very tail end; it has a nasty habit of getting finished, as do the guests shortly afterwards.

Red wines suitable for drinking with food can be divided into two types, firstly lighter bodied wines such as Beaujolais and the lighter bodied clarets, Bardolino and Valpolicello and secondly, fuller bodied wines such as the heavier bodied clarets (red Bordeaux), red Burgundy, Chianti and Rioja.

You can sometimes tell the type of wine – not the quality – from the shape of the bottle but you can be misled because shapes traditionally associated with certain renowned French wines are also now used for inferior wines from other countries. The very common shape shown in the first diagram overleaf, with straight sides and high shoulders, was originally an indication of wine from the Bordeaux region of France. It is now used for many varieties of wine some of which bear no resemblance to Bordeaux. (See diagrams overleaf for the shapes used for other types of wine.)

Left to right: 'Bordeaux' (see previous page); Burgundy; Rhine, Alsatian and Moselle; Chianti; Champagne and sparkling wines

Red wines are normally served at room temperature and it's a good trick to draw the cork out of them and leave them to 'breathe' for at least an hour before serving. This makes the wine much smoother in flavour and brings out its aroma much better.

The great classic French red wines – clarets and Burgundies – have white equivalents. White 'clarets' are known as white Bordeaux (Graves and Sauternes are the best known) and range from dry to really very sweet and can be drunk whenever you feel that kind of white wine is appropriate. The white Burgundies are extremely dry, with a 'flinty' taste, and are usually drunk only with fish dishes. Italy produces a lot of red wine, largely of a more full bodied type; and some good white wine, particularly from the north of Italy. Spain produces a large quantity of wine of, by and large, indeterminate character, often of great strength but not much subtlety. Some rather higher quality Spanish wines are now on the English market, notably some of the Riojas and Valdepenas, and these are much more reasonably priced than the great classic wines of France. Germany produces a great deal of very high quality white wine in tall, slim bottles with colourful labels and extremely long names. Usu-

ally, the longer the name the more expensive, and surprisingly the sweeter the wine. Hock, which comes from the Rhine Valley and is the richer, more fruity of them, is always in brown bottles, and Moselle, which comes from the Moselle Valley, and is a lighter, sharper set of wines altogether, normally comes in green bottles, although the shape is identical. If you don't feel terribly confident and expert, and don't have a good wine merchant who's interested in your return trade and not just the profit he can make on his first sale, it's not a bad idea to do what's done in Europe and to buy a branded wine such as Hirondelle. There are a number on the market, produced variously in France, Italy, Austria and Spain. Find one you like, and stick with it. There is a lot of expertise that goes into making sure that every bottle of the brand tastes pretty well the same when it's opened. Alternatively, choose from the selection offered at a chain store with a reputation for good value wine, such as Sainsbury's or Marks and Spencer. (A second label on Marks' wine recommends the correct temperature at which to serve that wine and foods appropriate to it.)

Whatever you serve, make sure that you have an alternative available. A surprising number of

SPARKLING WINES

Good   Not so good

SHERRY

Good   Not so good

people like a glass of water, whether mineral or tap, to clear their palates and help wash down the meal. Don't forget when you are laying the table to include a water glass for that, and provision for filling it, without having to get up and rush off into the kitchen.

The wine for the food
If you want to be traditional, perhaps for a very special dinner party, the classically accepted partnerships are:
with soup: dry sherry or dry Madeira
with fish: dry white wines or dry Champagne
with roasts or game: red Burgundy or full claret
with sweets: Sauternes or fine sweet hock
with cheese: Port, brown sherry or Madeira.

Helpful guidelines to follow are light wines before fuller ones; dry before sweet; white before red; lesser wines before fine ones. When one wine only is served throughout a meal it should be the wine most appropriate to the main course.

Dry white wines which stimulate the palate are good as an aperitif or with most starters. (Chablis, Muscadet, Portuguese Vinho Verde, Champagne or other sparkling wine if dry.)

Dry or medium dry white wines suit plainly cooked veal, chicken and fish dishes and drink well throughout the meal. (White Burgundy, Sancerre, Alsace Riesling, Moselle, Soave, Verdicchio.)

Rosé wines of a medium dryness are pleasant summer wines for cold plates and picnic dishes. (Tavel, Rosé de Cabernet.)

Lighter bodied red wine is pleasant with lamb chops, veal escalopes and milder casserole dishes

ALL-PURPOSE WINE GLASSES

Tulip (1)   Goblet   Traditional for Alsatian
and German wines

Tulip (2)   Balloon glass for   Traditional for
Right for table   brandy and fine red   claret
wine and brandy   Burgundy

(light clarets, Beaujolais, Valpolicello, Bardolino).

Fuller red wine suits red meats, rich stews, casseroles, game dishes (St Emilion and Pomerol among the clarets; red Burgundy, Côtes du Rhône, Chianti, Rioja).

Sweet white wines are drunk chilled, on their own or to go with certain sweet puddings and dessert fruits. (Sauternes, sweeter hocks, Muscat de Beaumes de Venise, etc.)

And how to serve it

1. All white wines should be served chilled, but not iced. Never put ice into them.

2. Most red wines are best served at room temperature, but since room temperatures vary, it is best to let them stand for a few hours in a 'comfort zone' of around 15–18°C (60–65°F). Never subject the wine to fierce, direct heat. Uncork red wines at least an hour or so before serving. Young ones up to 3 hours.

3. The purpose of decanting is twofold; to separate the wine from the lees and, with red wine, to let it take the air. Add to that the pleasure of the sight of wine decanted, whether in a decanter, a carafe or glass jug. It is not, however, *necessary* to decant red wine, so long as the bottle has stood still for an hour or so before serving.

4. Glasses for wine should be clear, colourless and thin. Some experts recommend a bowl that narrows towards the rim so as to hold the wine's perfume. And ideally it should be a stemmed glass, whether the stem is long or short. The glass should be big enough to swirl the wine around to release its fragrance and the glass should be filled only half way up or, at most, two-thirds. A 162–175-ml ($5\frac{1}{2}$–6 fl-oz) glass is a good all-purpose size.

Rescue Operations

When catastrophe strikes, and it usually does at some time or other, the first, most important and probably last real rule is *don't panic*! Firstly, if you don't panic, you can probably do something about it. Secondly, if you don't panic your guests may not even notice that anything is wrong, and thirdly, if you don't panic it's not going to spoil *your* evening. If you do, it may take you more than that night to recover your reputation as one of the great crafty hostesses.

As there is such a wide variety of things that can go wrong, there are no perfect solutions, but there are a few general guidelines depending on the problem.

Burning

If something's burnt, and burnt badly there is usually no way of rescuing it. The taste of singe goes right the way through, whatever it is, and that particularly applies to dishes with liquids, soups or casseroles. In this case see below for alternative strategies. If, however, something burns dry at the bottom of a pan and the rest of the things on top of it are still whole and unburnt, like potatoes, take the good food out of the saucepan without trying to scrape the remains off the burnt bottom until after you have put it into soak. That way, what you've rescued shouldn't have any taste of burning on it.

If the starter or main course is burnt . . .
If it's something like a roast that's really got quite charred on the outside, you can cut the outside away, and carve it in the kitchen, bringing it in ready cut on a plate. Or you can pretend you like your meat very well done! It all depends on how badly it's burnt and on you. But remember, you can't really cheat when something's burnt. The taste is unmistakable. So it's often better to revert to one of the instant alternatives. If it's a first course, try one of the quickie soups, like Tomato and orange, or scrambled eggs flavoured with whatever happens to come to hand – smoked salmon or a few herbs – piled on rounds of toast and served with a flourish.

If it's a main course that's irredeemable it depends to a certain extent on what you've got in the house. I usually keep a tin of tongue and a small tin of black cherries to hand just in case. The tongue can be taken out of the tin, thinly sliced, heated quickly in a baking dish in the oven (or under the grill); the tin of cherries goes into a saucepan with 10 ml (2 level tsp) arrowroot, blended with a little of the juice until it's smooth. Heat it through, it forms a bitter sweet sauce to go over the tongue, and save the dinner completely. It's a small investment for peace of mind.

If the pudding's charred . . .
If it's a pudding that's burnt, you may be able to rustle up a quick fruit salad made with fresh fruit rather than something out of a tin. Or cored, unpeeled *eating* apples sliced thickly and fried quickly and lightly in foaming butter, sprinkled with a little brown sugar, and with either cream or home-made custard all over the top. If you haven't got cream or home-made custard try a dollop of bitter marmalade or apple jelly in the middle where the core used to be.

A carton of good ice cream in the freezing compartment of your fridge or freezer will get you out of a lot of trouble. A tube of Rolos (chocolate toffees) melted together in a saucepan with just a drop of milk makes quite remarkable chocolate fudge sauce in the American style. Indeed, one of my American friends is so devoted to it, she always takes a couple of tubes home with her just so she can make it.

Under-cooking

If your problem is under-cooking and the food's not done, there are really only two solutions. Eat it raw or the one I favour is another round of drinks, a secret packet of salted almonds you happen to have kept hidden away somewhere to bring out for just an emergency like this, and keep the guests waiting until the food *is* done. Explain airily that the dinner is of such a delicate and sophisticated nature that it needs just a little longer to allow the aromas to blend perfectly.

Ways to hurry it up . . .

The alternatives depend on what you are dealing with. If it's a large joint, cutting it in half will speed up the cooking quite dramatically – again carve in the kitchen. If it's baked potatoes, a skewer through the middle will cook them through in a third less time. Turning the oven up a little has been known to speed up casseroles, but don't take this to extremes. A bottle of meat tenderiser can do wonders if the meat in a casserole just won't soften. Take it out carefully, sprinkle it with the tenderiser, let it stand for 5 minutes, put it back in the casserole and simmer for another 15 minutes or so, and it should be in melt-in-the-mouth condition. Be careful with the salt, though, if you do use a meat tenderiser to hurry things along, as it's pretty salty in its own right.

If you are faced with a cake type under-cooking problem – if it hasn't collapsed, the only thing to do is put it back in the oven, and wait until it *is* cooked. (In fact it is better to test things before they come out of the stable heat environment in which they are operating if they are at all fragile, like cakes or soufflés.) If the cake can't stand up on its own merits, I suggest you make instant trifle. In the case of a soufflé that's fallen, give up and do something else. There is no way of rescuing a sad-looking collapsed soufflé that I've ever heard of.

Rescuing a sauce

If you've got a sauce that's gone lumpy there are two things to do. One is to put it through a sieve, which effectively gets rid of the lumpiness. The other is to beat it until it is smooth. A liquidizer is one way of doing this, one of the crafty wire whisks is another.

If the sauce separates, it depends very much on what the ingredients are as to what the appropriate remedy is. But if it's a sauce that's been reduced a lot, very often half a glass of water will surprisingly both thicken and remake the sauce. It's often all the liquid having been cooked out that makes the oil and solids begin to separate. If you're making mayonnaise and it starts to separate, a tablespoonful of ice cold water followed by some more careful whisking will help to reform it. In more ordinary sauces, 10 ml (2 level tsp) cornflour blended in a little water, mixed in, can smooth out the most surprising troubles.

The key thing, when anything goes wrong, is to keep your nerve and to have a couple of alternatives available in an emergency store cupboard. I've given some ideas for this above. There are, of course, more expensive alternatives to have up your sleeve. A small jar of caviar to go as a topping for some scrambled eggs, a bottle of French white peaches in flavoured syrup, all look like they were the original intention and not a rescue operation.

I hope that most of the recipes in this book are pretty foolproof and shouldn't lead you into disaster, but if you do have that moment of terror, a quick look through the book might reveal quite a lot of dishes that don't take very long to cook at all. Either way, I hope that an evening that may have begun in disaster, finishes with compliments all round. The main thing yet again is to smile and look like you meant it all the time. That's what being crafty is all about!

Index

Note: Figures in italics indicate illustrations